Acknowledgments

I would like to thank the people whose contributions to my life have made the writing of this book possible. Reading *Telling Yourself the Truth* by William Backus and Marie Chapian, *Birthright* by David C. Needham, and *Building Your Self-Image* by Josh McDowell provided me with needed background material. I want to express my appreciation to my family for their support and help. My roommate, Juanita, has prayed for this book and has been very kind to its author. Not only did God use John Larson to inspire the basic format of this book but he and his wife, Linda, have been an encouragement to me. A special thanks goes to Michael O'Connor for proofreading this manuscript and sharing his deep insights into Scripture, which have not only influenced my writing, but also my life.

About the Author

LORRAINE PETERSON was born in Red Wing, Minnesota, grew up on a farm near Ellsworth, Wisconsin, and now resides in Guadalajara, Mexico. She received her B.A. (in history) from North Park College in Chicago, and has taken summer courses from the University of Minnesota and the University of Mexico in Mexico City.

Lorraine has taught high school and junior high. She has been an advisor to nondenominational Christian clubs in Minneapolis public schools and has taught teenage Bible studies. She has written four bestselling devotional book for teens:

If God Loves Me, Why Can't I Get My Locker Open?
Falling Off Cloud Nine and Other High Places
Why Isn't God Giving Cash Prizes?
Real Characters in the Making

Dying of Embarrassment
...& Living to Tell About It

LORRAINE PETERSON

BETHANY HOUSE PUBLISHERS
MINNEAPOLIS, MINNESOTA 55438
A Division of Bethany Fellowship, Inc.

Published by Bethany House Publishers
A Division of Bethany Fellowship, Inc.
6820 Auto Club Road, Minneapolis, Minnesota 55438

Printed in the United States of America

Library of Congress Cataloging-in-Publication Data

Peterson, Lorraine.
Dying of embarrassment & living to tell about it

(Devotionals for teens)
1. Youth—Prayer-books and devotions—English.
2. Identification (Religion)—Juvenile literature.
3. Self-respect—Religious aspects—Christianity—Juvenile literature.
I. Title. II. Title: Dying of embarrassment and living to tell about it.
III. Series.
BV4531.2.P488 1988 248.8'3—dc19 87-35334
ISBN 0-87123-967-1 (pbk.)

Preface

At a Saturday night prayer meeting, our leader, John Larson, excitedly shared with us the life-changing practise which he had learned from his friend Randy Nichols. I listened eagerly.

John's "secret" was this: He has learned how to spend his spare moments putting more and more of God's Word into his heart. "The neat thing is that you can build your spiritual muscles by constantly feasting on God's Word. On only one meal a day, you'll never be a healthy, robust Christian."

One of John's strategies is to carry memory verse cards in his shirt pocket. Even while climbing stairs at work, he has time to put a little of God's Word into his spirit. He gave us other steps for internalizing and applying Scripture, too.

Although I've been exposed to sound Christian teaching all my life, I had never been taught how to meditate on Scripture. I wish that I had begun reaping the benefits of systematically internalizing God's Word as a young person.

In the weeks that followed I wrote out verses on cards and took them with me to school. During each free period, I soaked in some more of the Bible. There were many times throughout the day when I could feed on God's Word: waiting for the bus, jogging, relaxing after dinner—even standing in line at the supermarket.

That summer I attended Bill Gothard's Basic Youth Conflicts seminar again and discovered he had a heavy emphasis on Scripture meditation. The most helpful idea he added to what I had already learned was: "Always fall asleep meditating on Scripture." I added this practice to my strategy, and it, too, has been a tremendous help to me.

At about the same time, I heard several sermons on *who we are in Christ.* It was a subject I'd never thought much about. I began to see that I had accepted many lies about myself, and that these lies had to be replaced with God's truth. For example, the Bible teaches that In Jesus you and I are new creatures, that we're free from condemnation, competent as ministers of Christ, and that we are winners. In fact, we're more than conquerors! Getting our identity straight will build a foundation for new patterns of thinking and action. I realized that if I had received this teaching as a young person, I could have experienced more freedom and joy throughout my Christian life. This book is the product of what God has been teaching me during the past two and a half years. I pray that it will bless the lives of many, many young people.

Lorraine Peterson

Contents

Before You Read This Book . . .

A handsome university student was talking to the guest speaker after church on Sunday evening. I couldn't help overhearing the young man's able defense of his participation in Kung Fu (a martial art) and noticed how he remained untouched as the dangers were pointed out to him.

Later, as I saw him standing alone at the front of the church, I asked him, "Why do you study Kung Fu?"

He was silent.

"Is it because you think that you're inferior, and this is your chance to be someone special?" I pressed.

Tears filled his eyes and he nodded.

On another occasion, I took special notice of a beautiful girl who started attending our high school Bible club. The other girls' counselor and I wondered what it would be like to have the homecoming queen in a Bible study. Later, my friend confided in me, "I can't believe it—that girl has more problems and feelings of inferiority than the others."

That Christians have difficulty seeing themselves as God sees them is no secret. Perhaps this lack of self-acceptance is more acute among young people. The root of many problems faced by teenagers is a feeling of inferiority, and great confusion regarding personal identity. The purpose of this book is to answer from a totally scriptural point of view that often-asked question, "Who am I?" "The truest thing about ourselves is what the Bible says."[1]

Once you have accepted Jesus as Lord and Savior, the Bible teaches that certain things are true in your life. As you discover what God says about you and incorporate these scriptures into your self-image, you become free to express your true personality—a unique and beautifully designed mirror, reflecting Jesus to the world.[2]

Perhaps in the maze of books being written about self-image and self-improvement, a fundamental principle of the Bible has been largely overlooked:

> "For our struggle is not against flesh and blood, but against the rulers, against authorities, against the powers of this dark world and against the spiritual forces of evil in the heavenly realms" (Eph. 6:12).

Although the person who knows Jesus has the special protection of the Holy Spirit, "with whom you were sealed for the day of redemption" (Eph. 4:30), opposing spiritual forces often attack the minds and emotions of Christians.

Consistently in Scripture, we see the devil in the role of accuser. He accused Job of following God just because it was a good prosperity trip. Zech. 3:1 describes a vision in which Satan was standing at the right hand of Joshua the high priest to accuse him. Rev. 12:10 reads like this: "For the accuser of our brothers who accuses them before our God day and night has been hurled down." In verse nine that person is identified as that great dragon, that ancient serpent called the devil.

Only God's truth can refute these accusations of the devil and free us to think of ourselves as God thinks of us. "Once you were alienated from God and were enemies in your minds because of your evil behavior. But now he has

---

[1]Josh McDowell, *Building Your Self-Image* (Wheaton, Ill.: Tyndale House Publishers, 1986), p. 129.

[2]If you or your family have a background of occult activities or participation in false religions, it would be wise to seek out a trusted Christian counselor or pastor who has a deep understanding of the demonic forces involved in such practices and their affect on people.

reconciled you by Christ's physical body through death to present you holy in his sight, without blemish *and free from accusation—if you continue in your faith, established, and firm,* not moved from the hope held out in the gospel'' (Col. 1:21–23).

This is not to say that we are merely robots who can think only the thoughts of the devil or of God. Prov. 16:1 explains: "To men belong the plans of the heart.'' Nor is it to deny that many of our problems are caused by willful disobedience to God's Word. If you decide to tell a lie, you have to live with the consequences of that falsehood—in fact, you've just opened the door for the devil to fill your mind with deceptive thoughts. Only repenting from that lie and telling the truth to any person who heard it can put you on track again. Lack of self-discipline, not allowing our spirits to receive instruction from God in order to tell our bodies what to do, is another problem. You can't brush off the fact that you drank three chocolate malts in a row on the first day of your diet with a simple, "the devil made me do it.'' The devil did not make you do anything. You did not control your body and help it to do God's will.

You should expect, however, that the devil will try to attack your mind and emotions. He will attempt to sow seeds of hate and discord. He will try to get you to misinterpret actions and words of other people. Most people will agree that it's not what happened to you, or your physical handicap, or the situation—it's how you view it that's the key to success or failure. And you see, it's rather in keeping with the character of Satan to order one of his tormenting demons to put lies into your mind regarding any problem, or situation you may be facing. Peter warns us all: "Your enemy the devil prowls around like a roaring lion looking for someone to devour'' (1 Pet. 5:8). He doesn't literally munch on Christians for supper—he just eats away at them with thoughts designed to destroy. You need to know how to handle these fierce attacks.

An example will help illustrate what I mean.

Let's say you've been invited to the birthday party of

the most popular boy in your youth group. It's to be a Saturday at his parents' lakeside cabin with swimming, boating, hiking, and a big picnic. You decide to spend your paycheck to get something really neat to wear. After hours of shopping you're completely frustrated. Why are all the sharp sports clothes made for slender people? The devil has been telling you all along that because you're overweight, you're ugly and unacceptable to others. You've always felt that you must have clothes that are outstanding to make up for all your deficiencies. But you can't find anything. Now, you're worn down to the point that Satan decides on a full-scale attack: "You've failed every time you tried to lose weight, so now you're fat and ugly and you have nothing decent to wear. The other kids won't accept you anyway. You might as well stay home."

You have three choices. You can agree with the devil's ideas, keep listening, and sponsor a full-scale "pity party." You can counter with a defiant "No! I'm good-looking, and maybe I like being more than skin and bones. I make up for it by my sense of humor. Everyone agrees that I'm personality-plus. I'll go to the party and I'll make myself the center of attention even if I go in rags." However, those defensive answers, though they seem positive, are only devil's food cake. The new lies about being superior might *taste* better, but they're still from Satan. *There is an alternative.* It's replacing the devil's lies with God's truth.

Begin the process of replacing false ideas with true ones by remembering how Jesus handled a similar situation.

When the devil tried to make Jesus doubt who He really was ("If you're *really* the Son of God—and maybe you're not—you must prove it in a spectacular way"), Jesus first recognized the devil's lie. So He made up His mind to stand against it. (James 4:7 tells us to do the same thing: "Resist the devil, and he will flee from you.") The reason Jesus could make such a firm stand against the devil was that He had no ungodly desires for comfort, popularity, power, or wealth that Satan could use to his advantage. Rev. 12:11 explains that this same attitude has enabled Christians throughout the ages to be victorious over the devil: "They overcame him by the blood of the Lamb and by the word of their testimony: they did not love their lives so much as to shrink from death."

Second, Jesus quoted God's Word to the devil, and He had a total commitment to doing the will of His Father, which gave the devil no loopholes. Never face the devil in your own strength. Just tell him (out loud if necessary), "Because Jesus shed His blood for me, I'm His and I am what God's Word says I am and I'm willing to obey Jesus no matter what it costs." The strategy Jesus used against the devil's attacks cannot be improved upon and it will work for you.

Now let's apply these tactics to the birthday party dilemma. Instead of entertaining the lies, feed on God's truth. Tell yourself something like this: "The devil is trying to tell me that outward appearance is everything. Well, I won't accept that because the Bible says, 'The Lord does not look at the things man looks at. Man looks on the outward appearance but the Lord looks at the heart' (1 Sam. 16:7). In fact, God, I've fallen into the popularity trap. I repent and ask forgiveness. I determine to be popular only with you. I'll go to the party and not worry about the impression I make. Oh, and there's another lie I see, too. I can go on a diet because God's Word declares, 'I can do all things through Christ who strengthens me' (Phil. 4:13). I will claim power from Jesus for losing some weight."

Thinking God's words, speaking them, and obeying them will change your life.

In order to let God transform your thinking, two things are necessary.

The first step is to start taking Scripture at face value. Jesus said: "Apart from me you can do nothing." Period. We have a tendency to revise and even to "correct" this type of biblical statement, until it reads, "People can do great things with just a little help from Jesus." We accept nearly every trend in modern thinking with a spoonful of

Christianity added. If we took God's Word seriously, we would not assume that psychological concepts (and these concepts differ greatly depending on what book you read and what theory you accept) fill in the gaps that Scripture does not cover. Instead, we'd remember that Jesus said, "When he, the Spirit of truth, comes, he will guide you into all truth" (John 16:13). Prayerfully seeking God's answers for the things we do not understand would be a lot safer than automatically swallowing the prescriptions the world is currently dishing out.

The second step is getting enough of God's Word into your mind and spirit so that you can successfully fight wrong ideas and mental attacks of Satan. Because he felt such a strong presence of evil, Martin Luther once threw an ink bottle at the devil. Using Scripture as your weapon, however, will not only be more effective, it will save the wallpaper in your room. How do you use the "sword of the Spirit," which is the Word of God? You need to make the Bible a part of you by learning to meditate on it and to fill your thoughts with it.

In his excellent booklet, "The Secret of Success,"[3] Bill Gothard lists the scriptural promises we can claim if we truly meditate on Scripture:

If you meditate on Scripture and obey it, God promises that

1. **You will enjoy success**
   "Do not let this Book of the Law depart from your mouth; meditate on it day and night, so that you may be careful to do everything written in it. Then you will be prosperous and successful" (Josh. 1:8).

2. **Whatever you do will prosper**
   "But his delight is in the law of the Lord, and on his law he meditates day and night. He is like a tree planted by streams of water, which yields its fruit in season and whose leaf does not wither. Whatever he does prospers" (Ps. 1:2–3).

3. **You will be wiser than all your enemies**

---

[3]Used by permission of Institutes of Basic Youth Conflicts, 1987.

"Oh, how I love your law! I meditate on it all day long. Your commands make me wiser than my enemies, for they are ever with me" (Ps. 119:97–98).

4. **You will be wiser than all your teachers**
"I have more insight than all my teachers for I meditate on your statutes. I have more understanding than the elders for I obey your precepts" (Ps. 119:99–100).

5. **You will be filled with joy**
"My soul will be satisfied as with the richest of foods; with singing lips my mouth will praise you. On my bed I remember you; I think of you through the watches of the night" (Ps. 63:5–6).

6. **Your success will be obvious to all**
"Be diligent in these matters; give yourself wholly to them, so that everyone may see your progress" (1 Tim. 4:15).

The Apostle Paul proclaims that renewing your mind will transform your life. And it's not surprising that this fact has been affirmed by scientific investigation. Dr. Paul Meier did an extensive research study that proved that "students who had practiced almost daily Scripture meditation for *three years* or *longer* came out, statistically, significantly healthier and happier than students who did not meditate on Scripture daily."[4] Dr. Meier concludes: "Daily meditation on Scripture (with personal application) is the most effective means of obtaining personal joy, peace, and emotional maturity."[5]

---

[4]Paul Meier, M.D., *Meditating for Success* (Grand Rapids, Mich.: Baker Book House, 1985) p. 22.
[5]Ibid., p. 24.

WEEK 1
DAY 1

How to Use This Book

We humans aren't noted for our ability to stick with something day in and day out, month after month, year after year. So we've set up a system to make it easier for you. Perhaps you noticed above the chapter title *Week 1/ Day 1*. We've divided the book into thirteen weeks of readings, with five readings per week (that way you won't get behind even if you miss a day or two). It's important that you regulate your pace through the book to get the most benefit from it.

Along with regulating your pace, the book also starts you out meditating on verses that tell you who you really are in Jesus. If you make these truths part of you, it won't matter whether the devil attacks you through pride or a terrible sense of inferiority. You'll have the truth and you'll be able to stand your ground. The idea is not to be the kid who can recite the most verses letter perfect to win a free ski trip to Colorado. Rather, it's to let God's Word become what you think about all day long.

Your Part

1. Make a card like the one shown in the book and carry it with you all day long.
2. Train your mind and spirit to absorb the verse during the natural breaks you have during the day, such as

- After meals.
- While waiting for the school bus.
- While driving—provided you can still be a safe driver.
- When the teacher gives study time at the end of class.
- During commercials while watching the football game on TV.
- While doing things that don't involve mental concentration like jogging, washing dishes, grabbing a bite to eat when home alone, drying your hair, bike riding.
- AND MOST IMPORTANT falling asleep meditating on the verse.

3. Ask someone else to check up on you to see if you are meditating on Bible verses every day. You and your best friend (or boyfriend or girlfriend) could go through the book at the same rate, make the cards, and report to each other. Or you could report to one of your parents, your youth pastor, or your Sunday-school teacher.

If you decide to use this book as a guide for establishing the life-long habit of meditating on Scripture throughout each day, it will be one of the most important decisions you've ever made. On the other hand, if you've never made Jesus the Lord of your life, nothing in this book will make sense. Only a new creature in Christ can completely receive God's Word as power capsules to live a new life.

WEEK 1
DAY 2

Stop!

If you've never invited Jesus into your heart to forgive your sins and to live inside of you as Commander-in-chief of your life, what you read in this book won't really help you. *But you can make that life-changing decision right now.* Here's how:

1. Realize that God really does love you and has a bright future planned for you, but that it has all been spoiled by sin.

2. Murderers and robbers and drug addicts aren't the only ones who have sinned. You have sinned, too—not only have you done wrong things, but your thoughts and motives have been impure. If you have your excuses, ask yourself this question: "Would you really be proud to have the whole world see the unedited movie version of your thoughts?" And most of all, you've ignored God and acted as if you could live just fine without Him. You can't get off the hook.

3. You cannot reach God or get to heaven by making New Year's resolutions or by trying to be good. Being *better* than someone else won't really help. Trying to be "good enough" for heaven is like trying to swim from California to Hawaii. The Olympic champion and the non-swimmer will both meet the same fate. If it were possible to board a ship headed for Hawaii, however, those who accepted the ride would be saved. Because none of us has

the hope of reaching heaven by our own efforts, Jesus became our "boat." Jesus died to wipe out your sins. He died to remake you into a new creature and give you free passage to heaven. Do you want to accept His gift to you?

4. In one way, the salvation Jesus offers costs nothing—no money, no good works to make up for the past. But in another way, it costs everything. You're giving up your whole life to Jesus—relinquishing the right to be the boss of your life. You must admit your sin and your need to ask forgiveness. Then you give Jesus everything you have—friendships, desires, leisure time activities, studies, and bad habits. Mere words will never impress God, but if you *really* want Jesus to run your life from now on, you can pray to God using these words—or some of your own which express this idea. "Dear Jesus, I know I have done wrong things and I am a sinner. Thank you for dying for me. Please forgive my sins and come into my heart to take over the control of my life. From this day on, I'm yours and my purpose is to do your will. Thank you for coming into my life."

PART 1

In Jesus I Am a New Creation

Therefore if anyone is in Christ, he is a new creation; the old has gone, the new has come.

2 Corinthians 5:17

WEEK 1
DAY 3

Don't Be a "Turkey"

There's an interesting story about an Indian who stole an egg from an eagle's nest and put it among the eggs of a turkey he was raising. When the eggs hatched, the other turkeys thought that a rather ugly member of their species had emerged. His wings were different from those of the turkeys, but no one taught him how to fly. Because he knew no other way to act, the eagle was scratching on the ground with all the turkeys.

One day an eagle flew overhead. How the displaced eagle wished to fly, effortlessly, like that soaring bird! The others laughed and said, "You're a turkey and a turkey can't fly." But his desire became even stronger. Deep inside, he knew he was missing out on something in life, and it made him miserable. Never chosen as a menu item for a feast day, he lived on and on with an unrealized dream in his heart.

Do you sympathize with the eagle who lived like a turkey? Is there something inside you that wants to be an Apostle-Paul-like Christian?

When you gave your life to Jesus and acknowledged Him as Lord—the One who has the right to rule your life—you became new on the *inside*. You now have new desires and new capacities. The only problem is that these are not visible to the natural eye. You still look the same. You live in the same environment. And your mental and emotional patterns appear to be fairly well established. If you don't concentrate on God's definition of a new creation in Christ, it's pretty easy for you to live like that eagle among the turkeys, experiencing constant defeat, discouragement, and frustration—all because you are unaware of who you really are. Instead of becoming a reality, the victorious life is only some longing deep in your heart.

But this doesn't have to be your biography. Someone has quipped, "It's difficult to soar with the eagles when you lived all day among the turkeys." But that person didn't take into account the dynamite power of the Holy Spirit in the life of new creatures in Christ. You need to know that you are no longer a turkey but an eagle with the supernatural energy to rise in joy and victory. When you fail, the devil's sarcastic, "You turkey!" may echo someplace back in your mind. Yet, you must stand firm.

Personalize Isa. 40:30–31: "I will hope in the Lord and renew my strength. I will soar on wings like eagles. I will run and not get tired. I will walk and not faint." You *are* a new creature. Let that new life unfold into something beautiful.

WEEK 1
DAY 4

A Tale of Two Apple Blossoms

Annie and Angie Apple Blossom were admired by all who passed by. Their exquisite beauty and delightful aroma were duly appreciated. Then one day, a lady cut Angie off the tree and put her in a beautiful vase with water. Both apple blossoms still looked identical, but there was a fundamental difference—Angie was self-sufficient, but Annie still depended on the tree for life. The lady felt bad when Angie turned into an ugly brown twig, so she put paper flowers on her. Now she looked good, but had no genuine life. Annie however, continued to receive life from the tree and produced apples. In the fall, she looked like a dead twig. She looked worse than Angie. But when spring came again, her blossoms were fragrant and alive—she was receiving life from the tree.

Annie and Angie Apple Blossom are like people today. Some are "dead in trespasses and sins" (Eph. 2:1) because they have no spiritual life. Others are totally dependent on *God-life*. They are new creatures. Like Angie Apple Blossom, people who are dead in trespasses and sins can display paper flowers and plastic apples, but they don't have everlasting life. On the other hand, people who are "born again" receive a new supernatural life from God.

When you declared Jesus to be the Lord of your life and accepted His forgiveness, you received life which comes from God himself. Only that God-given life can produce anything spiritual. "Remain in me and I will remain in you. No branch can bear fruit by itself; it must remain in the vine. Neither can you bear fruit unless you remain in me" (John 15:4).

When you accept Jesus, you become spiritually alive. The new you—the *real* you—is a spiritual being receiving constant life directly from God just the way Annie Apple Blossom receives her life from the tree. Sometimes your flesh (the part of you that isn't eternal) would rather have fake life. After all, artificial flowers usually *look* perfect and they, like other lifeless things, don't change or experience growing pains.

You really need to become acquainted with the new you so you can tell that "bod" of yours to bug off and permit you to live according to your spiritual life. First, you must realize that God's life within you has dynamite energy for victory and change, that God's life has powerful potential for plenty of peace and joy and love and all those good things you need.

However, your unrenewed mind, your stubborn will, your vacillating emotions, and your body's desires can put that God-life in a cage so it cannot express itself to others. Really allowing God's life to flow through you is so wonderful that it's worth any sacrifice you must make to enjoy its fruit.

The new you, filled with God's eternal life, really wants to follow Jesus even when your flesh protests. ("Stay home from Bible study and watch TV, I'm tired," or "Don't even try to love that girl—I don't like her personality.") The new you on the inside wants to show up on the outside.

The tale of two apple blossoms is intended to bring you back to a very old truth: Jesus is the vine and you're a branch receiving from Him your spiritual life that comprises the real you deep down inside.

MEMORIZE

"I am the vine; you are the branches. If a man remains in me and I in him, he will bear much fruit; apart from me you can do nothing" (John 15:5).

VISUALIZE

PERSONALIZE

Jesus is the vine and I'm His branch. I must remain in Jesus and allow Him to live through me in order to produce spiritual fruit. Without Jesus, I can do nothing.

PRAY THE VERSE, APPLYING IT TO YOUR LIFE

Dear God, thank you that Jesus is the vine and as a branch I get my very life from Him. Help me to stay in Jesus and permit His life to flow through me in order to produce fruit. Lord, without you I know I can't do anything, not even ______________________________ (a Christian activity you regularly engage in).

MEDITATE ON SCRIPTURE

Make a copy of this card. Use the card to meditate on this verse every chance you get throughout the day. Fall asleep thinking about this verse.

WEEK 1
DAY 5

Introducing the New You

Have you ever watched trapeze artists perform? They seem to be able to pull off acts that are superhuman. No one could get me to walk on a tightrope seventy feet above any cheering crowd. Balancing in midair atop three friends who could sneeze or stumble or flinch from insect bites is not my cup of tea. What if my mind wandered or the ladder broke?

But I enjoy watching trapeze acts because I admire two special qualities I see in these circus performers: They realize the full potential of human life in one small area; and they have learned to put their minds and bodies under the discipline required to achieve a higher goal. There's a lesson here that can be applied to your Christian life.

In order to live the abundant life that Jesus promised, you must learn who you really are in Christ. Furthermore, you must discover how to discipline your mind and body so that it becomes a help rather than a hindrance to living for Jesus.

Although you may feel like a "Doctor Jeckle-Mr. Hyde/Good Me-Bad Me" combination, you're not. The Bible says, among other things, that you are a "co-heir with Christ" (Rom. 8:17), "the salt of the earth" (Matt. 5:13), and part of a "chosen people, a royal priesthood . . . a holy nation" (1 Pet. 2:9).

Paul concludes his discussion of the conflict between

good and evil familiar in the experience of every Christian with the statement, "In my *inner being* [the new you] I delight in God's law" (Rom. 7:22). "Through Christ Jesus the law of the Spirit of life set me free from the law of sin and death" (Rom. 8:2). That's who he really was. His problem was that "the law of sin" using the parts of his body as allies was "waging war against the law" (Rom. 7:23) that he knew in his mind.

In other words, the new you deep down inside is capable of living free from the grip of sin through the power of the Holy Spirit. However, your flesh—the part of you that isn't eternal and which is used to sinning—will protest. The devil with all his lies will try to convince you that the new you wants to sin. Because your undisciplined mind would rather think about cute boys or beautiful girls than about Jesus, the devil will taunt, "See—you're not a new creature. You don't really love Jesus one bit and maybe you're not a Christian."

1 Pet. 2:11 clarifies what's happening: "Dear friends, I urge you as alien and strangers in the world [you're a spiritual being with citizenship in heaven], to abstain from sinful desires, which war against your soul." The cause of the conflict is a satanic attack against the new you, coordinated with habitual mental and physical responses to certain stimuli. *What are you going to do about these attacks?*

First, you keep searching the Scriptures and meditating on God's Word to know who you are in Christ. Just as the trapeze artist must remember who he is to keep from losing his nerve, you must never lose sight of God's definition of a new creature in Christ. Second, you must discipline your mind and your body. Paul urges, "Be transformed by the renewing of your mind" (Rom. 12:2). Fill your mind with God's truth to contradict Satan's lies and to break old patterns. He further explains, "I beat my body and make it a slave" (1 Cor. 9:27)—not to be sadistic, not to impress God, but to qualify for God's best. Don't let an unrenewed mind and an undisciplined body prevent you from expressing your spiritual self. Introduce the new you to everyone you meet.

MEMORIZE (Don't let your flesh say, "This verse is too long"!)

"His divine power has given us everything we need for life and godliness through our knowledge of him who called us by his own glory and goodness. Through these he has given us very great and precious promises, so that through them you may participate in the divine nature, and escape the corruption in the world caused by evil desires" (2 Pet. 1:3–4).

VISUALIZE

PERSONALIZE

His divine power has given me, _______, all I need for life and godliness through my knowledge of Him who called me by His own glory and goodness. Through these He has given me very great and precious promises so that through them I may participate in the divine nature and escape the corruption in the world caused by evil desires.

PRAY THE VERSE, APPLYING IT TO YOUR LIFE

Dear God, thank you for giving me everything I need for life and godliness so I can't say that the Christian life is too hard. Thank you that this power comes through my knowledge of Jesus who called me by His glory and goodness. Thank you, Lord, that the wonderful promises found in the Bible enable me to participate in the divine nature and run away from the bad things in the world like ______ caused by wrong desires.

PRACTICE A PROMISE

Participate in God's divine nature by letting Scripture change you. For example, give "love your enemies" a try. Instead of reacting with anger and resentment, let Jesus in you love the guy who always puts you down.

WEEK 2
DAY 1

But I Just Can't Change

Katie came from a tough home. Her father was an alcoholic and her mother was a nervous wreck. Because she couldn't stand any more hurt and disappointment, she became hard and indifferent. She kept her distance from most people.

One day Nathan remarked, "You're about as friendly as a statue. What's with you, anyway?"

Katie was offended. "Well, that's just the way I am. I can't change. You can take me or leave me."

Nathan was quick to explain, "I didn't mean to hurt you. I just want to help. I've been studying 1 Peter. There's a verse that says, 'For you have been born again, not of perishable seed but of *imperishable*, through the living and enduring word of God.' When you accepted Jesus, you became new. God put the seed of His everlasting life in you. It's just that you have to allow this God-given life to develop and grow and saturate your personality."

Can you identify with Katie? Do you wonder if you'll ever be able to change? Human personality is interesting and hard to track down. On one hand, a nervous breakdown, a tragedy, or falling in love can alter someone drastically. Yet, if you're a natural scatterbrain and have seriously tried to become cool, calm, and sophisticated, you've probably been very disappointed with the results. Without new circumstances, it's pretty hard to change—

that is, unless you plug into God's power system.

When you're tempted to moan in desperation, "I've tried and tried but I just can't change," there are some important things to remember. First, underneath your body, mind, will and emotions is your spirit. Deeper than the personality trait you don't like is the new you, the life of the Holy Spirit, which you received at conversion, living in your spirit. 1 John 3:9 declares that a Christian will change his or her actions because "God's seed remains in him."

Second, don't condemn yourself or receive condemnation from others. Rom. 8:1 declares: "There is *no* condemnation for those who are in Christ Jesus"—even if you have some unlovable characteristics. (The first two points are very important. If you think "I'm awful because I'm shy, and so I must force myself to be the life of the party," you'll fail.)

Third, ask God to show you if there is sin, lack of self-discipline, or unteachableness on your part. Acknowledge your sin or your bad attitude. Confess it and forsake it. Prov. 28:13 teaches, "He who conceals his sins does not prosper, but whoever confesses and renounces them finds mercy." Don't permit pride to steal a victory from you.

Fourth, ask God to identify and heal the scars and hurts from the past that interfere with change in your personality. Ps. 147:3 is especially for you: "He heals the brokenhearted and binds up their wounds." Claim it.

Last, pray constantly that God will "strengthen you with power through his Spirit in your inner being" (Eph. 3:16). Receive God's power—yours just isn't good enough. *PERSISTENT* faith based on God's Word can change the seemingly unchangeable. Too often we're like the guy who prayed, "Lord make me patient, but not now." We ought to be like the widow Jesus told about who kept coming until she received her answer. How about basing your life on Scripture and continuing in prayer so the new you shows up in your personality?

MEMORIZE

"And we, who with unveiled faces, all reflect the Lord's glory, are being transformed into his likeness with ever-increasing glory, which comes from the Lord, who is the Spirit" (2 Cor. 3:18).

VISUALIZE

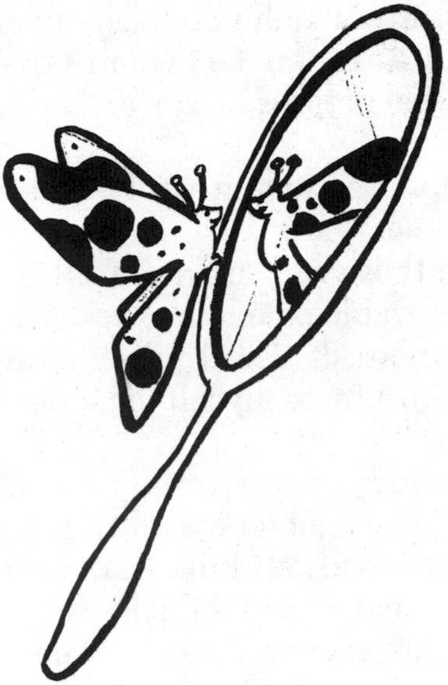

PERSONALIZE

And I, ________, reflect the Lord's glory. I am being transformed into His likeness with ever-increasing glory, which comes from the Lord who is the Spirit.

PRAY THE VERSE, APPLYING IT TO YOUR LIFE

Dear God, thank you that I reflect your glory. Lord, thank you that I'm being transformed into your likeness with ever-increasing glory, which comes from the Holy Spirit. Thank you, Lord, that you'll even change ________ (bad personality trait).

RECEIVE GOD'S VISION FOR YOU

Think of the thing you most dislike about your personality. Remember that as you yield to God, you are being transformed into the likeness of Jesus. Let God show you His plans for the new you.

WEEK 2
DAY 2

Operation Unlimited and the Failure of Fearful Freddy

Are you ready for a little science fiction?

Freddy from Centerville was always bothered by the limitations of being human. Why couldn't he fly, like the birds? Why couldn't he have a perfect computer memory? Why couldn't he speak whatever language he wished without having to study? Then he heard of a new breakthrough in modern science. By means of an operation it was possible to install a "new person computer chip" inside the human brain. By turning a switch, a person could disconnect his human brain and turn on a supernatural mind.

Freddy volunteered for what turned out to be a very successful experiment. By turning on the switch, he could be transported instantly to any place on earth, or to any planet. All his friends laughed at him, however, and called him weird, so he stayed in Centerville. When he used his new brain to get 100 on every Spanish test without studying, the teacher gave him a zero and accused him of stealing her tests. "Only a genius could get 100 on five tests in a row," Miss Strawmat insisted, "and I've taught you for two years. You don't qualify."

Freddy could have turned a switch and have become the star in any baseball game, but he was afraid. Because he had always been a klutz and had been teased so unmercifully about being the "strike-out king," he got sick to his stomach even thinking about stepping onto a baseball field again. So operation unlimited didn't significantly change the way Freddy lived because he was chained by the opinions of others and memories of past failures.

Fear kept Freddy from a new way of life.

Col. 2:13 tells us, "God made you alive with Christ." Verse 20 of that chapter goes on to explain: "You died with Christ to the basic principles of this world." Paul continues: "Since, then, you have been raised with Christ, set your hearts on things above. . . . Put to death, therefore, whatever belongs to your earthly nature" (Col. 3:1, 5). He concludes, "Therefore, as God's chosen people, holy and dearly loved, clothe yourselves with compassion, kindness, humility, gentleness and patience" (Col. 3:12).

Reading Colossians, one gets the idea that the new, supernatural dynamite power of the Holy Spirit is available to change every part of our lives and that we have a choice whether or not to use this power. "But," you may protest "if it's *that* simple, if the part of me that likes to sin really died with Jesus on the cross and I really have Christ's resurrection life in me, why do I seem to have so many problems?"

Maybe going back to the story of Freddy will help you. Like Freddy, you changed completely when you became a new creature in Christ—a new power became available to you. However, there are earthly chains that must be broken for this power to flow through you. The devil has used other people, society in general and sometimes even demon spirits to program you wrongly.

Let Jesus free you from the fear of what other people think and from the unwillingness to be misunderstood. Give Jesus the tangled emotions resulting from the traumas in your life. Allow Him to heal you and give you the wisdom to identify and resist the lies of Satan in problem areas. Recognize that thoughts of suicide, rebellion and self-hatred come from the devil. Permit the truth of God's Word to wipe out these destructive ideas.

As you allow Jesus to pinpoint and deal with the things that limit the expression of Jesus' resurrection life in you, He can change you from "Fearful Freddy" to "Courageous Christian."

MEMORIZE

"I have been crucified with Christ and I no longer live, but Christ lives in me. The life I live in the body, I live by the faith in the Son of God, who loved me and gave himself for me" (Gal. 2:20).

VISUALIZE

PERSONALIZE

I, ______, have been crucified with Christ. I don't live any longer, but Christ lives in me. The life I live in the body, I live by the faith of the Son of God, who loved me and gave himself for me.

PRAY THE VERSE, APPLYING IT TO YOUR LIFE

Dear God, thank you that my old life has been crucified with Christ. Thank you, Lord, that your life is living in me. Thank you that, although I live in a body, I live by the faith of the Son of God, who loved me and gave himself for me.

MEDITATE ON SCRIPTURE

Make a card like this one so you can think about his verse every time you have a spare minute. Go to sleep repeating the verse in your mind.

WEEK 2
DAY 3

Princes, Diamonds and Matilda

In the Kingdom of Kantu there was great excitement. Why? The queen had just given birth to identical twin boys. These sons of the king grew up knowing that great riches and authority were automatically theirs. They had done nothing to earn their position—it all came from their father.

Although the two boys enjoyed the same birthright, they were very different. One was lazy and selfish, while the other studied diligently, tried to understand the problems of the people of his kingdom and sought advice from wise and learned men. Irresponsible and shiftless, the first son was a poor representative of his father. In contrast, the other acted and talked like a storybook prince.

If you have given your whole life to Jesus, then you, like the twins, have received a great birthright. Only yours is better because it came from God himself. Just because you have God's riches and His power at your disposal doesn't mean you can go on a life-long vacation, though. It's up to you to take advantage of all that God has given you.

Another way of illustrating this same principle is to think of Christians as diamonds that reflect God's light. "God . . . made his light shine in our hearts" (2 Cor. 4:6). The intrinsic quality of a diamond is revealed in its ability to reflect light. Because Christians receive the entire "new creation package" as a gift from God, we can take no credit. And just as the value of a diamond is dependent on the number of facets and how it is cut, our response to Jesus, the master diamond cutter, determines what others will see in us. Only those who submit to God and permit Him to chisel away wrong attitudes and bad habits can truly reflect God's light to the best advantage.

Realizing who you are in Jesus and cooperating with Him to allow His life on the inside of you to show up on the outside is different from trying to reach some vague objective using faulty information. As you'll see when you consider the actions of Matilda Jones.

All her life, Matilda had heard it would be nice to learn to swim. But she'd also heard that no one in the Jones family had ever succeeded. Maybe it was too much to expect, but Matilda felt it her duty to try. Each day she spent time in the shallow pond near her house, kicking her feet and waving her arms vigorously until exhaustion forced her to quit. She tried harder and harder but finally decided her family was right.

Are you a "Matilda" Christian? Have you been told that there are no Christians who reflect God's love, joy and peace, but that you should try hard because it's a worthy goal? Or do you know who you really are—a child of God, with His life of power inside you? Do you realize that you're like a diamond, capable of relecting God's light to the world? Do you check out what the Bible says so you can correctly cooperate with God in order for His life to show up in yours? Let princes, diamonds and Matilda teach you something that Paul said best in Col 1:27: "To them, God has chosen to make known . . . this mystery, which is Christ in you the hope of glory."

MEMORIZE

"Continue to work out your salvation with fear and trembling, for it is God who works in you to will and to act according to his good purpose" (Phil. 2:12-13).

VISUALIZE

PERSONALIZE

I, ______, will continue to cooperate with God so that I can work out what He has worked in me. God's power within me to fulfill His purpose won't show up in my actions unless I cooperate with Him.

PRAY THE VERSE, APPLYING IT TO YOUR LIFE

Dear God, I ask you to help me cooperate with you. I determine to obey you so your life inside me will show up on the outside. Thank you that you work in me to do your will. In ______ (difficult situation) I will work with you to accomplish your purpose.

ATTACK A PROBLEM IN YOUR LIFE

From Scripture, find three things you must do to cooperate with Jesus so His new life inside you can eradicate that eyesore on your Christian testimony.

WEEK 2
DAY 4

Caution: Con Man in Control

It was a rather unlikely scheme but it worked. One night as the president and owner of a large company was working late in his office, he was suddenly surrounded by the night watchman and his mobster friends. They beat him up, broke his glasses and took him to a cellar outside the city.

After three days without food or sleep, the president was accosted by the night watchman. "Sign this paper or I'll kill you!" he shouted. The president had no way of knowing that in the house across the road there was a meeting of F.B.I. agents and that one scream would have freed him within minutes. Unable to see without his glasses and too weak to think straight, he signed a paper that put his company under the authority of the night watchman.

But surely this story should have a happy ending—right? The watchman must go to jail and the man who spent forty long years working for his position should once again sit in the president's office. Real life doesn't always read like a novel, sad to say.

There are Christians in the same position as that company president. Maybe you're one of them! Although they're really new creatures in Christ, the devil has tricked them to the point that they feel totally helpless and miserable.

Although powerful religious leaders and the whole Roman empire were against them, New Testament believers were undaunted. When Paul and Silas arrived in Thessalonica, people came crying to the city authorities: "These men who have caused trouble all over the world have now come here" (Acts 17:6). Paul's attitude was, "If God is for us, who can be against us?" (Rom. 8:31). Paul even wrote to the Corinthians, who were less than shining examples of what Christians should be, "He will keep you strong to the end, so that you will be blameless on the day of our Lord Jesus Christ. God, who has called you into fellowship with his Son Jesus Christ our Lord, is faithful" (1 Cor. 1:8–9). There was recognition of the power of the Holy Spirit alive in the believer to overcome any obstacle that might come up.

Now let's go back to the con man and his bag of tricks. Why did the company president fall into his trap? First, he was all alone, away from friends who could help. Taken by surprise, he let fear get the upper hand. He permitted his present state of weakness to blot out the big picture. Finally, he was ignorant of the facts.

Satan uses all these tactics to try to keep you from reaching your new creature potential. If you don't get Christian fellowship and try to be a Lone Ranger Christian, you're open to attack. You also need to digest a lot of "fear not" verses and put them to work in your life, because fear always opens the door to the devil. Remember the *whole picture*: God is God and He is *always* in control. Meditate on this fact frequently so Daniel-in-the-lions'-den faith can be yours when the devil tries to convince you that your fender-bender accident is indeed the end of the world. Study your Bible diligently, asking the Holy Spirit to show you truth. "Be still, and know that I am God" (Ps. 46:10) can blot out your I-can't-live-in-this-house-one-more-day attitude. Don't let the master con man rob you of your new creature identity.

MEMORIZE

[Jesus] replied, "I saw Satan fall like lightning from heaven. I have given you authority to trample on snakes and scorpions and to overcome all the power of the enemy; nothing will harm you" (Luke 10:18, 19).

VISUALIZE

PERSONALIZE

I, ______, have authority from Jesus to trample on the devil and his schemes. Jesus gives me His power to overcome my enemy Satan. Nothing will harm me.

PRAY THE VERSE, APPLYING IT TO YOUR LIFE

Dear God, thank you that you have given me authority over the devil and the power to overcome. Thank you that nothing, even ______ (present concern or danger) will harm me.

COLLECT ON YOUR "NEW LIFE" INSURANCE POLICY

It reads "nothing will harm you," not even the thing you fear the most. Use your power to trample on Satan. Tell him in the name of Jesus to get lost.

WEEK 2
DAY 5

Wishy-Washy Wishes vs. Deepest Desires

Debbie attended the Saturday night youth rally and heard a stirring pep-talk on the verse, "Whoever loses his life for me will save it" (Luke 9:24). Because the speaker ran out of time before getting to the "will save it" part of the verse, it sounded as though Debbie would have to give up everything she enjoyed to follow Jesus. Debbie pictured herself in the middle of Swaziland, hundreds of miles from the nearest pizza parlor, working among a tribe that considered it a disgrace for a woman to pick up a ball or wear blue jeans, doing the worst thing she would think of—caring for war victims in a hospital. Although she loved Jesus an awful lot, Debbie wondered if she could stand it in Swaziland.

Sunday morning, her pastor preached on the verse, "Delight yourself in the Lord and he will give you the desires of your heart" (Ps. 37:4). By the end of that sermon, Debbie was nearly ready to pray for a new red sports car with Dolby Stereo. However, the two messages left her so confused she didn't even bother.

Have you, like Debbie, had problems reconciling "deny yourself" verses with passages like Ps. 145:19: "He fulfills the desires of those who fear him"?

Let's start unraveling the dilemma by making an observation about human desires. Although Charlene Chocoholic's craving for candy may be very strong, there is a hidden desire somewhere deep inside to fit into a size nine and to have her friends exclaim, "You look so good since you lost weight!" Even if Adam has a surface wish to hurt and embarrass his parents by running away from home, underneath all that is a longing to be part of a happy family with a loving mother and father.

Let's go a step further. Who are *you*? Are you just a bundle of physical and psychological needs? A person who will *die* if you can't play baseball? Someone who gets depressed if blueberry malts are unavailable? A chick who can't exist without a boyfriend? Or are you something a lot deeper—a person with the very life of Jesus flowing through you?

In Greek there are two words for *life*. Interestingly enough, the *life* we are to deny comes from a root word whose meanings include, "to be tossed with a tempest," "to be troubled," "to be scattered with a whirlwind." This word pictures a bunch of restless desires that, even though granted, don't bring peace. On the other hand, the *life* Jesus gives comes from a root word meaning, "to flow" or "pouring like rain"—a life force with steady power!

To a person who doesn't have the supernatural life of Jesus flowing from within, making the team, being a cheerleader, buying new clothes, having a good time, or impressing other people is all there is to life. And although the *F* on the geometry test may be forgotten within two weeks, it signals the end of the world today. The winds of circumstance dictate everything, and there is no anchor.

The flowing quality of Jesus' life in you can drive out the tempestuous whirlwind type of life with its temporary desires. When you find that you really want something a lot, it's a good idea to ask God, "Is this a temporary desire of my flesh, or is it a real desire of my new life?" Give it some time. God wants to fulfill all the desires of the new you, as you delight in Him. He won't ask you to go against the true personality He put inside you. But you need His help in discerning the difference between wishy-washy wishes and the deepest desires of the new nature Jesus gave you.

MEMORIZE

"I have come that they may have life and have it to the full" (John 10:10).

VISUALIZE

PERSONALIZE

Jesus came so that I, _______ , may have His ever-flowing new life and have it to the full.

PRAY THE VERSE, APPLYING IT TO YOUR LIFE

Dear God, thank you for coming to give me new life. Thanks for being the fountain of life with a constant fresh supply that enables me to have abundant life. Show me the things in my life that only belong to this temporary life and block the flow of your supernatural life. Show me if _______ is a wishy-washy wish or a true desire of my new life.

TERMINATE YOUR TANTRUMS

Stop the fits you stage whenever God, or some other person, doesn't give you what you want. Make a list of the longings of your heart and pray about them every day this week. Ask God to show you which ones are "new you desires" and which ones are wishy-washy desires.

WEEK 3
DAY 1

Self-Examination

1. If my body wants to watch TV instead of going to Bible study, I should
   ____ a. Take a cold shower to punish my body.
   ____ b. Make popcorn to eat while watching television.
   ____ c. Recognize that the new me deep down inside, who has eternal life, desires the Bible study more than the TV program, and tell my body, "You're going to Bible study."
   ____ d. Watch the half-hour program I like best and go to Bible study late.

2. Why is it sometimes hard for me to follow God even though I'm a Christian?
   ____ a. My mind and body aren't disciplined to help the new me follow God.
   ____ b. The devil is using his lies, combined with my old habitual mental and physical responses to convince me that I want to sin.
   ____ c. I don't fully realize what it means to be a new creature in Christ.
   ____ d. All of the above.

3. Which is *not* a step in changing the unchangeable?
    ____ a. Understanding that your spirit, which is deeper than your body, mind, will and emotions, is the real you.
    ____ b. Confess sin, lack of self-discipline and unteachableness.
    ____ c. Ask God for inner healing and receive God's power for change.
    ____ d. Repeat "I'm a success and I can do it" thirty-six times.

4. No Christian ever really reflects the life of Jesus, but I should still try hard. T F
5. A Christian can reflect the life of Jesus if he or she cooperates with the new life inside. T F
6. What tricks does the devil use to rob me of my new creature identity?
    ____
    ____
7. What was your last big failure? ________________
8. What things that you learned in this chapter can help you *not* to fall into Satan's trap? ________________
9. What verse are you going to memorize and internalize to help prevent future failure?
    ____ a. 1 Cor. 10:13.
    ____ b. 2 Cor. 5:17.
    ____ c. 1 John 4:4.
    ____ d. Other (specify) ________________.

10. How do I determine if a wish is really the desire of the new me deep down inside? ________________

1. c. **2.** d. **3.** d. **4.** F. **5.** T. **6.** Isolating me from fellowship, startling me, getting me to concentrate on my present weakness instead of seeing the whole picture and setting my mind on God's power, keeping me ignorant of the facts. **7.–9.** Personal. **10.** I keep praying and checking the desire with God's Word. Carnal desires come and go, and they don't line up with the Bible.

PART 2

In Jesus I Am Showered With Kindness

Through him and for his name's sake,
we received grace.

Romans 1:5

WEEK 3
DAY 2

Oops! I Just Got Hit Over the Head With a Ton of Kindness!

Judy, a cheerleader, was one of the most popular girls at school. She had asked some of her friends to a pool party on Saturday afternoon. Elated to get an invitation, Sally offered to bring a cake for the supper.

She spent most of her Saturday looking through frosting recipes and making a cake from scratch. Her heart sank, however, as she opened the oven door. Instead of the high, fluffy layers she expected, she was faced with two slightly burned pancake-like circles! Although she valiantly attempted a double recipe of "lemon supreme frosting," the heat and the humidity made her icing thin and runny. Her frosting-covers-a-multitude-of-sins formula had failed. The end product resembled an aerial view of a balding blond hippie whose long locks failed to compensate for what he was lacking on top.

Thoroughly discouraged, she nervously dressed for the party, wondering what Judy's friends would say about her cake. She drove to Judy's house. Getting out of the car, she tried to balance the cake, her swim suit, a towel and her hairdryer in one hand as she closed the car door with the other. The cake slipped and plopped, top-side down, onto the sidewalk.

Teary-eyed, Sally was ready to climb back into the car and go home when she felt Judy's arms around her. "Don't worry about the cake," she comforted. "I'm just glad *you* made it to my party."

Sally could hardly believe it! There was no blaming. Just acceptance and love. Sally felt like a new person. She went in and enjoyed the party.

God's grace is like that—the type of mercy and kindness that can remake a person. One traditional definition of grace is "God's unmerited favor." It seems to me that all of us know we're unworthy of all God has done and wants to do in our lives. In fact we concentrate so much on being unworthy that we receive very little of God's grace. You see, God's grace is not only something that saves sinners from hell, it also has, according to one Bible dictionary, these definitions: *favor, kindness, friendship, God's forgiving mercy, gifts freely bestowed* and *Christian virtue.* And the Bible talks about receiving God's grace on a continuing basis!

You're probably missing out on a lot that God wants to give you. Learning to receive God's grace will change your self-image considerably—not to mention your attitude toward life. The testimony of a former accomplice to murder is this: "By the grace of God, I am what I am" (1 Cor. 15:10). That man was the Apostle Paul. What God's grace did for Paul, it can do for you.

Why not let God hit *you* over the head with a ton of forgiveness, kindness, mercy, favor and all those good things?

WEEK 3
DAY 3

Telling the Truth to the Devil

LeRoy spends hours in the lotus position trying to meditate just right to achieve "oneness with the universe." Kathy passes out flowers and asks for donations from sunrise until sunset without questioning her leaders. Ken goes door-to-door every day, whether he feels like it or not, in order to try to convert people to his religion. Cindi has piled up enough good works to fill a grain elevator and continues to volunteer for every charitable organization that will accept her services.

The sad part is that none of these people feels certain that he or she has done enough to please God.

If you take a course in comparative religions, you'll make an interesting discovery. The major thing that differentiates true Christianity from the other religions is *salvation by faith based on grace*—God's willingness to show His mercy and kindness in order to save us, even though we don't deserve it.

Titus 3:5 tells us ". . . He saved us, *not because of righteous things we had done, but because of his mercy.* He saved us through the washing of rebirth and renewal by the Holy Spirit." Jesus died for our sins. By His blood our sins are washed away. When we give ourselves totally to God and invite the Spirit of Jesus to live inside us, we become new people in Christ Jesus.

It's not a matter of trying harder. It's being remade by

accepting something supernatural—the forgiveness of God and a new boss for your life; Jesus living inside of you and making you different.

If you have accepted Jesus into your life, don't ever forget that you're saved by grace, made righteous by faith, and kept safe in Jesus by the mighty hand of God. Consequently, the devil has absolutely no business telling you that you might as well quit being a Christian because you're not good enough for God. The little sneak will even come up with things like this: "Hey, you lied. So now you've lost your salvation forever." If Satan tries these tricks, just tell him the truth: "Of course I'm not good enough for God, but He wants me anyway. Right here in 1 Tim. 2:3–4 it says, 'God . . . wants *all* men [in Greek usage this refers to the entire human race] to be saved." Or say, "Look here, Mr. Devil, 1 John 1:9 says, 'If we confess our sins, he is faithful and just and will forgive us our sins and purify us from all unrighteousness.' Lying was wrong. But I can confess my sin and receive forgiveness."

If you don't want to be another casualty, find out God's truth in His Word and tell the truth to the devil. Never let Satan try to talk you out of receiving God's grace.

MEMORIZE

"For it is by grace you have been saved, through faith—and this is not from yourselves, it is the gift of God—not by works, so that no one can boast" (Eph. 2:8–9).

VISUALIZE

PERSONALIZE

I have been saved by grace through faith. I don't earn God's grace and His favor. I receive it as a gift from God. I can't brag about what I'm doing or have done. All the credit belongs to God.

PRAY THE VERSE, APPLYING IT TO YOUR LIFE

I thank you, God, that I have been saved by grace through faith. I thank you that I have received your free gift of salvation and don't have to suffer insecurity attacks which make me worry that I'm not good enough for you. Lord, I thank you that I don't have anything to brag about and I don't have to constantly worry about my performance.

WEED OUT WILLPOWER CHRISTIANITY

List the areas where you've been trying in your own efforts to be good enough for God—or to measure up to your own expectations or those of others. With a red pen write over each item on your list, "I will receive the grace of God by faith. I will let Jesus live His life in me."

WEEK 3
DAY 4

The Dream That Came True

It was only a dream but it was fun while it lasted.

Because Tom stuttered, he'd always had a fear of meeting new people. In his dream, he had to enter a room full of strangers and introduce himself to each one of them. He was terrified. Even more frightening to him was a command from the sky: "You must witness about your faith in Christ to someone in that room." Tom felt that was unfair for God to ask him to witness—that should be a job reserved for self-assured jocks. Just then a beautiful white dove landed on his shoulder and kindly began to speak: "Don't worry. I'll help you. I love to see people break out of old patterns and conquer their hang-ups. Just go and ask the first person his name and tell him yours."

Tom did it, even though he stuttered a lot.

"That's fine. You did your best," cooed the dove. Encouraged, Tom continued and things went smoother.

Then the dove explained, "You ask this man how things are going and his reply will give you an opportunity to tell him about Jesus."

Tom obeyed. Although he hesitated several times and forgot the Bible verse he wanted to use, the man listened. The dove smiled, "That's wonderful. You're learning to be a witness for Jesus."

The good news is that God's grace—His favor, kindness, and mercy—is with you just like that dove that sat on Tom's shoulder. It's there if you listen to the Holy Spirit, the Comforter, and don't chase Him away by accepting one of the devil's lies ("You never do anything right"; "You're not good enough to witness for Jesus"; "You flubbed it again—better give up"). The Bible says, "The Lord loved the righteous" (Ps. 146:8)—not "the Lord loves the righteous if they make no mistakes and if they are cool." "The Lord bestows [gives] favor [grace] and glory"—not just to His pets but to those who follow Him.

The psalmist continues, "No *good* things does he withhold from those whose walk is blameless" (Ps. 84:11). If you are following Jesus with all your heart, God's kindness, favor, grace and mercy are yours twenty-four hours a day. God's grace can be yours when you get a traffic ticket, when the teacher gives a pop quiz, and when you get blamed for what your little brother did. It's possible to sense so much of God's care and acceptance that these things don't throw you. By receiving God's grace and the power of the Holy Spirit, Tom's dream can come true for you. You can escape from the prison formed by your fear. You can reign in life because there will always be enough of God's grace for you to be on top of things.

MEMORIZE

"How much more will those who receive God's abundant provision of grace and the gift of righteousness reign in life through the one man, Jesus Christ" (Rom. 5:17).

VISUALIZE

PERSONALIZE

How much more will ______ who received God's super supply of grace, favor and kindness, plus the gift of doing what is right, rise above life's circumstances through Jesus Christ.

PRAY THE VERSE, APPLYING IT TO YOUR LIFE

Dear God, I *will* receive your never-ending supply of grace and kindness for ______ (problem of the day) and your gift of living right for ______ (difficult temptation facing you). Lord, I receive your grace so I can live like a king or queen who reigns over life's circumstances through the power of Jesus.

MEDITATE ON SCRIPTURE

Make a copy of this card and carry it with you through the day. Meditate on the verse every opportunity you get. Fall asleep thinking about the verse.

WEEK 3
DAY 5

Extra! Extra! Kindness Kills Pride, Greed and Bitterness!

Jennifer always said exactly what she thought. She might as well have been wearing a "nobody's-going-to-push-me-around" button. Strong-willed, she had trouble getting along with authority figures.

After receiving an *F* on a geometry test, Jennifer stood up and screamed, "You're the worst teacher I've ever had! You don't even know your subject and your explanations stink."

Instead of angrily writing out a discipline report and telling Jennifer he didn't have to put up with supersnots, the teacher soothingly responded, "Jennifer, please come after school tonight. I want to help you with the things you don't understand. I have confidence in your ability to get a good grade on the next test."

To her surprise, Jennifer felt tears fill her eyes. She heard herself say, "I'm sorry. I didn't mean it. I'll come in tonight for some help."

Kindness captures another victim!

Of course, the story could have had a different ending. Jennifer could have rejected the teacher's offer and continued in her rebellion. Like that teacher, God shows us His grace in order to get us to change our attitudes. In Rom. 2:4, we find a very important question, "Do you show contempt for the riches of his kindness, tolerance, and patience, not realizing that God's kindness leads you toward repentance?" God doesn't shower you with kindness, grace and forgiveness so you can go on sinning. God *hates* sin, and sin will separate you from God. His great mercy is meant to produce true repentance in you—not a casual "I'm sorry," but a renouncing of sin and a complete turn-around in the way you live.

The purpose of God's grace is to get you to confess that you have failed in your attempt to live life on your own. God wants to bring you to the place where you constantly cry out to Him for more of His kindness, favor, mercy and strength. We were designed to live each day completely dependent on the grace of God. But there are many attitudes that can prevent you from receiving His grace.

If you water down God's biblical commands so you can live up to them, you eliminate the need for God's grace. But God does not change His rules or lower His standards. Instead, He gives you the supernatural power of the Holy Spirit. His constant encouragement, favor, kindness and forgiveness enable you to live on a higher plane.

There's another way that you can lose out on God's never-ending supply of grace. James 4:6 tells you how: "God opposes the proud, but gives grace to the humble." Your attitude of pride, independence and self-sufficiency will keep you from receiving God's grace. Until you realize that you desperately need God's help *all the time for everything you do and everything you say,* you'll only have room for a little bit of God's grace.

Maybe it's materialism, or too much emphasis on achievement that is keeping you from the grace of God. In a whale's stomach, Jonah realized an important truth. "Those who cling to worthless idols forfeit the grace that could be theirs" (Jonah 2:8). You can be so busy doing your own things and so greedy for possessions that you have no time to receive anything from God.

Yet, probably the easiest way to miss out on the grace of God is to harbor bitterness in your heart. The bitter person becomes so hard that nothing can sink in. The devil tries hard to get you to become bitter, because then you'll miss the best thing in life—the grace of God. Repent of your sin and accept all the kindness and favor God wants to give you. Only then will pride, greed and bitterness be defeated in your life.

MEMORIZE

"See to it that no one misses the grace of God and that no bitter root grows to cause trouble and defile many" (Heb. 12:15).

VISUALIZE

PERSONALIZE

I, ______, will make sure that I don't miss the grace of God. I will not let any root of bitterness grow in my life and hurt me and others.

PRAY THE VERSE, APPLYING IT TO YOUR LIFE

Dear God, I want your grace and I need it. If I'm missing out, show me why. I repent over my bitterness about ______ and ______. Lord, I don't care whose fault it is. I forgive and I determine not to let bitterness in my life hurt me and others.

BANISH BITTERNESS

Ask God to show you if you have any roots of resentment in your life. Not only ask forgiveness but ruthlessly tear out any bit of bitterness.

WEEK 4
DAY 1

Is God Wearing His Happy Face Today?

Perhaps you've read the book, *Call of the Wild.* It's about a dog named Buck. Beaten constantly by his master and nearly starved to death, Buck was rescued by a man named John Thornton. In return for the genuine love and care he received, Buck willingly risked his life for his master. There wasn't anything Buck wouldn't do for John Thornton.*

God has done so much more for you than John Thornton did for Buck. He sent His only Son to die for you so you could be saved from hell. He constantly sends His love and grace and mercy and blessing your way. He has a wonderful plan for your life plus forever in heaven with Him. Who wouldn't want to obey a God like that? Rom. 12:1 says it well: "Therefore I urge you brothers *in view of God's mercy,* to offer your bodies as a living sacrifice, holy, and pleasing to God, which is your spiritual worship."

When you realize the depth of God's grace and kindness and mercy, you'll want to obey Him. In fact, you'll count it a joy to give up something for Jesus. Instead of letting the devil constantly condemn you for not measuring up as a model Christian, meditate on the grace of God. Receive the grace of God. Every day expect to see more of God's kindness, favor and mercy in your life. Constantly thank God for His grace, and things will change.

The kind of change that will come about is explained for us in Col. 1:6: "All over the world this gospel is producing fruit and growing, just as it has been doing among you since the day you heard it and *understood God's grace in all its truth.*" The more you experience of the riches of God's grace, the more natural your Christian obedience and outreach will become. The devil knows this, so he wants to hide this fact from Christians.

To show you what I mean, let's return to our dog, Buck. Let's imagine that a ghostlike being called "Hercamore the Horrible" was able to inject thoughts into Buck's mind. Hercamore's line goes like this: "John Thornton doesn't *really* love you. He's just showing you all this kindness to lead you into a trap. He's going to take all the fun out of your life. In fact, he's so strict that you can never please him no matter what you do. Don't trust him. Why don't you bite him right now before he whips you?" If Buck listened to all this garbage and acted on it, he'd soon feel like he was out of John Thornton's good graces—even if John Thornton loved him just as much as ever. Because of his thoughts and actions, Buck would feel guilty and, consequently, would be uncomfortable in his master's presence.

In the same way, the devil tries to feed us lies and get us to act on them so we can no longer enjoy God's grace.

As a loving master, John Thornton would have to try to straighten out Buck's thinking and punish him for biting, hoping that Buck would respond so he could continue to enjoy the love of his kind master. When you swallow the devil's lies that you're no good, that it's impossible to please God, that He's a Big Meany anyway so you might as well go and sin some more—God in His compassion must show His stern face. After all, a kind person doesn't smile and cheer as he watches someone edging closer to a dangerous cliff.

Whether you're seeing God's happy face or God's frowning face depends totally on whether or not you're letting His grace transform your life. From your point of view, is God wearing His happy face today?

MEMORIZE

"Consider therefore the kindness and sternness of God: sternness to those who fell, but kindness to you, provided that you continue in his kindness" (Rom. 11:22).

VISUALIZE

PERSONALIZE

I, ______, will recognize that God shows me both sternness and kindness. He will show me sternness if I reject His grace, because He must warn me of my danger. God shows kindness to me if I continue accepting His love and mercy in my life.

PRAY THE VERSE, APPLYING IT TO YOUR LIFE

Dear God, I thank you for your kindness and for your sternness that warn me of danger and disaster. Keep me close to you and keep me from falling so I don't need to experience your sternness. I receive your grace and mercy and kindness and plan to do so every day.

STOP AT THE RED LIGHT!

Check your life for warning signals. Have you been ignoring God's caution signs and consequently missed seeing His smiling face? With sincerity, write a letter to God, telling Him what you plan to do about those flashing red lights designed to protect you from more trouble.

WEEK 4
DAY 2

When Thinking Could Be Hazardous to Your Health

What kind of thoughts do you think about yourself? Where do these thoughts come from? Your self-assessment has tremendous potential for good or evil.

Of course, there's the "Positive Peter" type who stands in front of the mirror for hours proclaiming, "I'm super-intelligent and I'm the handsomest boy in my class." However, he still gets *D's* in algebra and hasn't succeeded in reducing the size of his ears and broadening his shoulders. Only in his dreams do hoards of girls run in his direction.

On the other hand, "Humble Henrietta" sprinkles her conversation with "I know *I* can never learn to drive a car"; "I make a lot of mistakes and will try harder next time"; and "I need to wear a lot a makeup—it helps hide my face." Somehow people fail to see her as a billboard advertisement for true humility.

The problem is that the devil has a special strategy for getting people to think of themselves in a wrong way. He'll dish out superiority or inferiority, whichever lie you'll swallow. In Rom. 12:3, Paul, who says the grace of God made him a new person, explains something he had learned. He says, "For by the grace given me I say to every one of you: Do not think of yourself more highly than you ought, but rather think of yourself with sober judgment, *in accordance with the faith God has given you.*" Faith to think of yourself in the right way comes from God and His

Word. "Consequently, faith comes from hearing the message, and the message is heard through the word of Christ" (Rom. 10:17). The idea is that you must get your opinion of yourself from God.

When you overhear your mom confide in the neighbor lady, "Liz is hopeless when it comes to housework—you're so lucky to have Vicky," do you get hurt and angry? Or do you ask God, "What is the real truth about me?" As you glare at the *D−* on the civics test you got back, does this thought cross your mind, "I'm the dumbest one in my whole family, and I might as well give up"?

Instead of garfing it up, remember that the Bible says, "I always thank God for you because of his *grace* given you in Christ Jesus. *For in Him* you have been enriched in every way—in all your speaking and in all your knowledge" (1 Cor. 1:4–5). Decide to reject the devil's lies. And when some lightning bolt from outer space suddenly descends with, "I'm the handsomest young guy in our church—any girl who gets some of my attention should count her blessings," don't let your mind wallow in daydreams based on that thought. Recall that God says: "Man looks at the outward appearance but the Lord looks at the heart" (1 Sam. 16:7).

You'll never be emotionally and spiritually healthy if you don't let God define who you are. Send Satan's thoughts back without opening the package.

MEMORIZE

"You then, my son [daughter], be strong in the grace that is in Christ Jesus" (2 Tim. 2:1).

VISUALIZE

PERSONALIZE

I, ______, will be strong, not in attempting to pat myself on the back while putting others down, but in the favor, kindness and mercy that I get from Jesus. I will not weaken myself by believing lies from the devil that belittle me.

PRAY THE VERSE, APPLYING IT TO YOUR LIFE

Dear God, I receive your strength. I know that the reason I can be strong in ______ (situation in which you feel weak) is because Jesus has a never-ending supply of grace just for me.

MEDITATE ON SCRIPTURE

Make a duplicate of this card to carry with you today. Use spare time to memorize and think about this verse. Fall asleep meditating on the verse.

WEEK 4
DAY 3

Switch Stations—and Listen to Something True!

It was one of those days. Nothing was going right. The history teacher was lecturing on the dreadful exams he was in the process of grading.

"Don't you guys ever study?" he asked. Gathering momentum, he continued, "Somebody even wrote that the French and the Indians fought against *each other* in the French and Indian War!" That somebody was Jason, and he listened more intently as the teacher ranted on.

"Any student who even listened for ten minutes, or read the book, or did the homework would know that in American history, with the exception of the Iroquois, the Indians were *allies* of the French."

Jason had listened in class. He had read the book. He had handed in his homework. He thought, "How can I be so dumb?" *Attack time!* The devil got out his "you're-worthless-and-should-drop-out-of-school" record and played it in Jason's ear.

Across the room sat Heidi. She hadn't heard one thing the teacher or anyone else had said all morning. The words her father had spoken at the breakfast table kept ringing in her ears: "There's nothing to keep me here. I'm leaving for good." Although Heidi's parents had always argued a lot, she had thought her dad cared about her. But he must not. Insecurity overwhelmed her. *Attack time!* She kept hearing Satan's sonata in demolishing Minors, entitled "You're Not Good Enough for Anybody to Love." She couldn't find an off button anywhere.

Do you ever feel like the main character in a similar plot? If so, read on.

There *is* an off switch when the devil starts attacking your mind. It's found in James 4:7: "Submit yourselves, then, to God. Resist the devil, and he will flee from you." First, you resolve to think the thoughts that Jesus would want you to think. Then you tell the devil in no uncertain terms to get lost in the name of Jesus. Tell him that the blood of Jesus protects you because you're God's child and he has no right to keep up the mental torture. Next, you must get out of the danger zone by running to Jesus and *receiving* from Him.

Although most Christians relate to the idea of telling God what the problem is, many don't really expect answers. You may suffer from some of the mental blocks that keep people from receiving all the love and comfort and wisdom God wants to give us. The Bible tells you—in more than one place—that God gives grace (favor, kindness, friendship, mercy) to the humble. You need to learn to receive God's grace.

If any of the following obstacles keep you from receiving from God, remember that in Jesus there is power to overcome them. You may have been taught independence and self-reliance to the point that you don't want to ask for help, even from God, unless there's an emergency. And because of this you're missing most of what God wants to give you. Maybe you feel you've let God down so you don't deserve anything. Realize that God doesn't dish out His kindness on the merit system. God gives grace to the humble. Maybe you've perceived the Christian life as plowing ahead in obedience without ever stopping to get some special encouragement from God. Don't forget that God is love and He wants to share himself with you. Perhaps you've experienced so little love and caring from people and you're so accustomed to life without tenderness and concern that you've never even thought of asking God for a "heavenly hug," or listening for all the ways He says, "I love you." But the Bible says that God "heals the brokenhearted and binds up their wounds" (Ps. 147:3). Let Him heal your emotional scars.

You can only get out of Satan's mental hell if, after resisting the devil, you run into Jesus' arms. Tell Him your problems and *receive* His love and His answers. You can switch stations and spend your life listening to God's truth instead of Satan's lies.

MEMORIZE

"Let us then approach the throne of grace with confidence, so that we may receive mercy and find grace to help us in our time of need" (Heb. 4:16).

VISUALIZE

PERSONALIZE

I will come before God, who sits on a throne of grace—a God who delights in showing mercy and love and favor and kindness. I will come to God with confidence no matter what the problem is. I will find understanding and caring and God's answer to my dilemma.

PRAY THE VERSE, APPLYING IT TO YOUR LIFE

Dear God, I'm coming to you as you sit on your throne of grace. I come to you with confidence asking mercy for _______ and help for _______. I expect to find what you have promised to give.

EXERCISE THE RIGHTS OF HEAVENLY CITIZENSHIP

Picture God on His throne of grace giving out mercy and kindness to His subjects. From Scripture promises you know, write a "Believer's Bill of Rights," remembering that the devil can't take any of these away from you. Are you exercising the rights that God gives to you as His child?

WEEK 4
DAY 4

Are You Trying to Grow in the Wrong Kind of Soil?

Brad had been a Christian for three months. He hadn't gone out drinking with his buddies or smoked marijuana or experimented with cocaine once in all that time.

But he was very lonely. He couldn't find a new gang of friends. He really didn't feel he belonged anywhere. Because the kids at church all came from Christian families, they didn't seem to understand him or the problems he was having.

One day, his former best friend, Dave, came driving by. "Hey, Brad, let's go pig out at McDonalds." So lonely he'd jump at a chance to go bird-watching at 4:00 a.m., Brad hopped into the car and they were off. Dave took him to the McDonalds on the other side of town—and there was the old crowd. Stuck without a ride home, Brad was forced to go with them.

Of course there was a kegger at Brian's house with all the beer you could drink and plenty of pot to go around. After five Cokes and an incredible amount of teasing, which was no longer good-natured, Brad joined in with the others. Arriving home late that night, he felt horrible. The devil whispered, "God will never forgive you now. There is no way to get the old joy back. Don't ever go to that church again. It's no place for bad guys like you."

Brad needed to know what Paul told the Romans:

We've been justified by faith and "have gained access by faith into this grace in which we now stand" (Rom. 5:2). What is this grace? It's favor, kindness, friendship and God's forgiving mercy. It's so fantastic that "where sin increased, grace increased all the more" (Rom. 5:20). It's God's wonderful characteristic of forgiving those who sincerely confess and picking them up and putting them on their feet again. It's grace like that which melts our preoccupation with self and makes us want to follow Jesus always.

But this grace isn't just for the Brads who blow it big—it's for every Tom, Dick and Hannah who talks back to his/her parents, who has trouble reading the Bible and who feels very unimportant and overlooked. The apostles knew this, and they constantly reminded people of the grace of God. Out of the twenty-two letters, or epistles, that are included in the New Testament, *sixteen* begin with something like, "Grace, mercy, and peace from God the Father and Christ Jesus our Lord" (1 Tim. 1:2). *Fourteen* end with a similar statement, and 2 Peter closes with the admonition: "Grow in grace." Paul and Barnabas told their converts to "continue in the grace of God" (Acts 13:43). Have you ever wondered why there is such emphasis on reminding people of the grace of God?

To answer this question, let's start with an example from nature. It's obvious that any living thing needs the right atmosphere in order to mature properly. How would you feel if your mom threw the plant you gave her for Mother's Day in a vase with some stones and put it in the darkest corner of the basement and left it? Even your kid brother, who has never studied biology, could tell you the fate of such a plant. A dog that's constantly kicked and mistreated won't make a good pet, and children who are not loved become maladjusted.

In the same way, a Christian who doesn't continually live in the consciousness of God's friendship remembering His mercy, meditating on His kindness, looking forward to His favor, and thankful for God's forgiveness—

will never be healthy spiritually. Once you've accepted Jesus, you're to grow in the soil of His grace.

A plant with good soil and just the right amount of sunshine and rain doesn't have to exert great effort to attain the right height; it just gets taller. Why don't you continue in God's grace and grow up spiritually?

MEMORIZE

"But grow in the grace and knowledge of our Lord and Savior Jesus Christ. To him be glory both now and forever" (2 Pet. 3:18).

VISUALIZE

PERSONALIZE

I will grow in the soil of God's grace, favor and mercy and in the knowledge of my Lord and Savior Jesus Christ. I will give Him glory and praise now and always.

PRAY THE VERSE, APPLYING IT TO YOUR LIFE

Lord, I ask you to show me how to constantly receive your grace and kindness. I ask you to teach me more about yourself. Then I know I'll grow into a healthy Christian. Lord, I praise you and give you glory.

MEDITATE ON SCRIPTURE

Copy this on a card and take it with you to meditate on during any spare minutes you may have. Go to sleep thinking about this verse.

WEEK 4
DAY 5

Self-Examination

1. How many times this week did you remind yourself that you're a new creature in Christ? ____ Did remembering this fact give you any victories? ________
2. Did you ever slip into thinking that your body, your emotions, or your mind was the real you? ____ What verse will you internalize to counteract this lie?
   ____ a. Gal. 2:20.
   ____ b. Rom. 6:11.
   ____ c. Col. 3:9–10.
   ____ d. Other (specify).

3. I deserve God's grace. T F
4. God loves to show kindness to people who don't deserve it. T F
5. Which is a great hindrance to receiving God's grace?
   ____ a. Bitterness.
   ____ b. Greed for possessions.
   ____ c. The devil's lie that God is a Big Meany who will never accept you no matter what you do.
   ____ d. All of the above.

6. Which one of the above-mentioned hindrances is *your* biggest problem? ________

7. Because God loves to show kindness and mercy
   ____ a. He doesn't punish sin.
   ____ b. He shows His stern face when you do something wrong, because in His mercy He wants to warn you of the consequences.
   ____ c. He is very lenient and lets His children get by with murder.
   ____ d. He sees only the good things you do and ignores the bad things.

8. Where do I get the answer to the question, "Who am I?" ________
9. Describe the soil of God's grace. ____________________

   ____

   Are you growing in that soil or in some self-made desert where you depend only on your own resources?

   ____

   How can you grow in grace? ____________________
10. Why not stop and ask God for some of His love and mercy and kindness right now?

1.–2. Personal. **3.** F. **4.** T. **5.** d. **6.** Personal. **7.** b. **8.** From what God says in the Bible. **9.** The soil of God's grace provides forgiveness for sin, mercy for mistakes, and love, kindness, favor and friendship to encourage us every day. I need to consciously remember that God is just waiting to shower His grace on me. I must meditate on scriptures that tell of His grace. **10.** Sounds great to me!

PART 3

In Jesus I Am Righteous

In him we might become the righteousness of God.

2 Corinthians 5:21

WEEK 5
DAY 1

The Best Trade You'll Ever Make

The newspaper headline caught Jane's eye: "Volunteer Serves Prison Sentence for Gang Leader." And she began to read the unbelievable story of a lawyer who had invested his time and money to help teenagers in New York City. When a tough gang leader robbed a bank, the lawyer dug out a two-century-old law that was still on the books and arranged to serve the time in jail so the boy could go free.

"I'm seventy years old," the lawyer explained, "and I've lived my life. I want Frankie to be able to live his."

When asked how he felt about having his freedom, Frankie quipped, "It's great. Now I can rob banks and Mr. Warwick can sit in jail."

It's a heartwarming story—until you find out how it ends. Something is wrong. Frankie should say, "This act of kindness has deeply touched my life and has made me decide to be an honest man." It just doesn't make sense that someone should take the rap for him so he can enjoy right standing with the law while he continues to be personally corrupt.

It seems that some people view Jesus' death for our sins exactly the way Frankie perceived the sacrifice Mr. Warwick make for him.

The Bible teaches: "God made him who had no sin to be sin for us, so that in him we might become the righteousness of God" (2 Cor. 5:21). Like the lawyer in the story, Jesus took your place. He suffered the penalty of your sin so that God can count you as righteous—*perfect*—in His sight. You, who deserve hell like everyone else in the human race, can go to heaven because Jesus died in your place. No matter how many times you hear it, never fail to appreciate the wonder of what Jesus did for you.

But the account of Jesus' death for you doesn't end like the one about Frankie and the lawyer. Jesus didn't die so you could keep on sinning your way to heaven. The promise that "in him we might become the righteousness of God" means more than God viewing us as sinless because Jesus died to erase all imperfections. It implies a change on the inside so profound that it transforms our attitudes and actions. It isn't only receiving God's forgiveness and righteousness by faith in order to get saved from hell; it's constantly appropriating the righteousness of Jesus by faith. It's saying, "Jesus, I can't love that person, but by faith I'll reach out in kindness trusting you to supply the love." It's obeying your mother with the faith that God will change her unreasonable attitude and protect you in the meantime. Receiving God's righteousness isn't a whitewash job that only covers up all the muck. It's a total exchange. You give Jesus your sin and He gives you His righteousness. It's the best trade you'll ever make.

WEEK 5
DAY 2

Do You Know the Secret?

Dawn felt stained and dirty. She was overcome by guilt and hopelessness. She had never wanted to have sex with her boyfriend, but when he said, "I can't stand a relationship in which I'm not free to express my love. Either we go all the way or we break up," she gave in. She just couldn't bear the thought of losing him.

And now she was more confused than ever. She still didn't want to let Dennis go. She figured that since she'd already wrecked her life, she might as well go on sinning. God seemed very far away and everything she'd learned at church became one big blur.

Dawn needs to discover the true meaning of the verse that changed the life of Martin Luther so many years ago. Maybe you do, too. It is Rom. 1:17: "For in the gospel a righteousness from God is revealed, a righteousness that is by faith from first to last, just as it is written: 'The righteous will live by faith.' " A sin addict needs two things: to get free and clean in the first place and then to stay that way. This is where "righteousness that is by faith from first to last" comes in.

First of all, Dawn needs to repent and by faith receive the forgiveness and righteousness Jesus has to offer. She must claim Rom. 5:1 as her own: "Therefore, since we have been justified through faith, we have peace with God through our Lord Jesus Christ." Someone has defined *jus-*

tified like this: "just as if I'd never sinned." Dawn needs to realize that "you've-wrecked-your-life-so-you-might-as-well-keep-sinning" is one of the devil's lies. She must accept the fact that once she has truly repented, she is totally clean in the eyes of God. She is free to live a new life.

That's the beginning of God's righteousness. But you not only become righteous by faith. You stay righteous by faith. After this, Dawn needs to meditate on God's Word so she can receive more and more faith in the areas that caused her downfall in the first place.

She must have faith that she can live just fine without Dennis because she can hold on to the promise: "The Lord is my shepherd. I shall lack *nothing*" (Ps. 23:1). She needs to decide that God can plan her future better than she can because His Word is true: " 'For I know the plans I have for you,' declares the Lord, 'plans to prosper you and not to harm you, plans to give you hope and a future' " (Jer. 29:11). And she must have the faith that she can say no to future temptation no matter how weak she feels, because she can stand on this promise: "He will not let you be tempted beyond what you can bear. But when you are tempted, he will also provide a way out so that you can stand up under it" (1 Cor. 10:13).

Dawn needs to know the truth. The root of her sin is not "everybody's doing it," or "she was lonely," or "she didn't think her parents really loved her." She sinned because of lack of faith.

There is a solution that will work for Dawn—and for you. It's a secret that has been printed in the world's best-selling book for centuries: "The just shall live by faith." Do you know that secret? Does it govern your life?

MEMORIZE

"And everything that does not come from faith is sin" (Rom. 14:23).

VISUALIZE

PERSONALIZE

I know that my sin comes from lack of faith. When I ______ (sin you committed), I did not have faith that God could ______.

PRAY THE VERSE, APPLYING IT TO YOUR LIFE

Dear God, thank you that faith comes from you and your Word. Thank you that as I meditate on your Word, I can build my faith. Help me to remember that sin comes from lack of faith.

INSTALL SOME MORE FAITH IN YOUR HEART HOUSE

Make a list of your faithless acts. Are worrying, complaining, anger, self-pity, and selfishness on the list? How could real faith that God is in control eliminate these? Determine to hide a lot of God's Word, the source of faith, in your heart.

WEEK 5
DAY 3

But You've Got to Build the Dam!

Stephanie had heard her mother's scolding a thousand times and she could repeat it verbatim: "Stephanie, you're lazy and undisciplined. Your room is a disgrace. You always put off your schoolwork until the last minute and then do a sloppy job. Just look at you! Sixty pounds overweight and eating a candy bar!" Most of the time Stephanie politely stared at her mother as she tuned out the words. But this time she listened and felt terrible. Alan, the neatest guy in school as far as she was concerned, had told her something that really made her start thinking. "Stephanie," he had said, "if you'd lose weight, you'd be the prettiest girl around."

Later, as she thought it over, she realized that Jesus was looking down from heaven at her. Being overweight didn't just affect her status with Alan, it hurt her testimony. And she really did want to be her best for Jesus. How could she get that "bod" of hers to cooperate so she could do the right things?

Two passages of scripture come to Stephanie's rescue and will give you some help as well. Rom. 8:13, 14 explains: "But if by the Spirit you put to death the misdeeds of the body, you will live." This verse tells us that our spirits—receiving instruction and power from the Holy Spirit—are to rule our bodies. The "whatever-comfort-I-want-I'll-get" approach is as wrong as the "super-self-denial-torture-my-body-into-submission" technique. As a person who has received God's righteousness, you must live by the faith that the Holy Spirit has the plan and the power to make your bod a servant to your spirit.

The other passage is Rom. 6:13: "Do not offer the parts of your body to sin, as instruments of wickedness, but rather offer yourselves to God, as those who have been brought from death to life; and offer the parts of your body to him as instruments of righteousness." By faith, relying on the power of the Holy Spirit, tell your bod that it will eat tossed salad and fish instead of cupcakes, potato chips and chocolate bars so it will be in better shape to serve God. Make 1 Cor. 10:31 part of you, knowing that God never gives commands without supplying obedience power: "So whether you eat or drink or whatever you do, do it all for the glory of God."

Realize that when you give in to laziness, you become the devil's ally. And if you think this is too strong, read Prov. 18:9: "One who is slack in his work is brother to one who destroys." Instead of getting down on yourself, remember that you're a new creature in Christ and that "the righteous shall live by faith." Believe that God can show you organizational skills and make you a good worker. Let Prov. 14:23 permeate your spirit and your personality: "All hard work brings a profit." Believe it and live by it.

An illustration might clarify the point. Your body, mind, emotions and will are somewhat like the destructive flood waters of spring. They can't go unchecked, or they wreck everything in their path. To avoid the annual disaster, it's essential to put faith in an engineer and his plan for a dam and make the necessary sacrifices to build it. Once the rushing waters are under control, they become an asset. You must believe for big changes and willingly endure whatever pain is necessary to place your body, mind, emotions and will under the domination of the Holy Spirit to aid you in obeying God. But you've got to build the dam no matter what the cost. You can't permit your mind and emotions to run wild. The Holy Spirit must be the designer of that dam because your blueprints, like those of millions of others who tried out their own ideas, will fail.

MEMORIZE

"Therefore, I urge you, brothers, in view of God's mercy, to offer your bodies as living sacrifices, holy and pleasing to God—which is your spiritual worship" (Rom. 12:1).

VISUALIZE

PERSONALIZE

Because God showers me with undeserved favor and kindness, it is only right that I give my body to Him—to do anything He wants me to do any time He wants me to do it. That's my way of showing God my devotion and giving Him honor.

PRAY THE VERSE, APPLYING IT TO YOUR LIFE

Dear God, thank you for your mercy. In appreciation for all you've done for me, I'm telling my body to ______ (something you know is God's will but that you'd rather not do). This will be my way of saying that I love you and adore you.

ENROLL THAT BOD OF YOURS IN A SPIRITUAL EXERCISE CLASS

Write out some directions for your body: For example, "Mouth, you'll stop complaining about Mr. Triangle's geometry class." Then thank Jesus that He'll give you supernatural power once you decide to cooperate with Him.

WEEK 5
DAY 4

Open the Package

Derrick was a new Christian who came from a family with no verbalized religious convictions. When he confessed that he had no idea how a Christian should act, someone suggested that he read the Ten Commandments and the Sermon on the Mount.

As he read, Derrick examined his life. He had never worshiped any images and he thought he could stop lying. Stealing wasn't a temptation for him and he assumed he could give up swearing. But the command "Honor your father" really blew his mind. The Sermon on the Mount laid it on even thicker—"Love your enemies and pray for those who persecute you" (Matt. 5:43). Derrick didn't know if he could even tolerate his stepfather—to say nothing of loving him.

You see, Derrick was an illegitimate child who didn't even know his real father. When Ed married Derrick's mother, he resented the boy and took everything out on him. He was the center of most of the arguments his parents had. This made Derrick insecure and he blamed his stepfather. Feeling that Ed was out to get him, Derrick had grown to hate him.

Do you face a similar situation? The answer is wrapped up in these few words: "The righteous will live by faith." Derrick, first of all, must forget about trying to love his stepfather in his own strength. The clenched-fist determination to be kind and helpful and loving produces nothing but frustration. However, putting faith in the fact that God's power is working will bring about results. God has given us His promise, "For it is God who works in you to will and to act according to his good purpose" (Phil. 2:13).

By faith, Derrick can rely on the strength and wisdom of the Holy Spirit as he attempts to put Luke 6:27, 28 into practice: " 'But I tell you who hear me: Love your enemies, do good to those who hate you, bless those who curse you, pray for those who mistreat you.' " By faith Derrick can ask God, "What extra special nice thing can I do for my stepfather?" And when he realizes that the answer is something like cleaning out the garage without being told, he can decide immediately to make the sacrifice necessary to complete the task.

Derrick's stepfather may remark, "Your school grades are bad, and you'll never amount to anything anyway." Derrick, empowered by the Spirit, can use the next available opportunity to tell his friend, "My stepfather is a very intelligent man and a hard worker. He just became vice president of the company he works for." And Derrick can pray for his stepfather every day.

The neat thing is that as you obey by faith, God works a miracle in you—He changes you into the person who can obey His commands from the heart. By faith you rise out of the temptation to try to lower God's standards so you can live up to them. And by faith you receive His supernatural power to live a supernatural life. "Those who receive God's abundant provision of grace and the gift of righteousness reign in life through one man, Jesus Christ" (Rom. 5:17).

Ability to live right is a gift. Receive it by faith and open the package.

MEMORIZE

"However, to the man who does not work but trusts God who justifies the wicked, his faith is credited as righteousness" (Rom. 4:5).

VISUALIZE

PERSONALIZE

If I don't strive in my own strength but trust God who makes me righteous, my faith puts real righteousness into my bank account because it allows God not only to forgive me but to change me.

PRAY THE VERSE, APPLYING IT TO YOUR LIFE

Dear God, thank you that I don't have to depend on my ability to be good but on your goodness. I have faith so that you will put your righteousness in me so I can please you by ______ (doing something that you find difficult but know is a command of God).

MEDITATE ON SCRIPTURE

Copy this card so you can study it throughout the day. Let God put the verse deep into your spirit and learn more about justification by faith. Repeat the verse to yourself as you fall asleep tonight.

WEEK 5
DAY 5

Don't Even Bother to Watch the Devil's Parade

Lashonna woke up from her dream, pondering the strange circumstances manufactured by her subconscious.

She had dreamed that she had fallen in love with a fine Christian young man named Aaron and had promised to marry him after he graduated from the university he was attending out-of-state. As soon as Aaron left for college, another man began to relentlessly pursue her. He was extremely good-looking, an olympic champion and a multi-millionaire. He tried everything. He bought her a new car and left in it her driveway; he offered to take her on a trip around the world accompanied by the chaperone of her choice; he bought a mansion where she would live if she married him.

Before she met Aaron, she would have jumped at the opportunity to enjoy such wealth and to share life with a famous person. But now she couldn't care less. Nothing he did impressed her in the least. She was in love with Aaron. She trusted him and looked forward to marrying him. Her actions were totally based on faith in the word and character of a man she wouldn't see for months. Lashonna only wanted to please Aaron and prepare herself to be his wife.

As Lashonna thought about her dream, she began to understand what her Sunday-school teacher was trying to get across. He had said, "The part of you that likes to sin really died when Jesus died on the cross two thousand years ago. When you accept this fact by faith, receive God's forgiveness and invite Jesus into your life, you experience the resurrection life of Jesus." He had quoted Rom. 6:5: "If we have been united with him in his death, we will certainly also be united with him in his resurrection."

Her teacher had explained that, although the devil with his carnival of sinful activities will always be around to tempt everyone, the person who by faith counts himself dead to sin won't even want to sin. Instead, he or she will be anxious to please Jesus. Rom. 6:17 puts it like this: "But thanks be to God that, though you used to be slaves to sin, you wholeheartedly obeyed the form of teaching to which you were entrusted. You have been set free from sin and have become slaves to righteousness."

Lashonna could now understand it more clearly. When she accepted Jesus as her Savior, she gave herself to Him like she had promised herself to Aaron in her dream. If she continued to really believe that Jesus loved her and that His plans for her were better than her own, the devil's ideas would be totally unappealing. By faith she could pass up the chance to date the non-Christian Olympic champion, because pleasing God was more important and Jesus had something better for her anyway. The faith that God's strength was hers could give her the courage to ask forgiveness of the person she offended. Faith that God can even cover failure could keep her from cheating on the final exam she didn't get a chance to study for.

"The righteous shall live by faith" (Rom. 1:17). And part of that faith is that you are "dead to sin"—that watching the devil's parade of wrong actions and attitudes doesn't really interest you anymore because you're a new creature. It's only when you lose faith in who you are in Jesus that jealousy or anger or selfishness look appealing.

The resurrection life of Jesus is much more exciting. Don't even bother to watch the devil's parade.

MEMORIZE

"In the same way, count yourselves dead to sin but alive to God in Christ Jesus" (Rom. 6:11).

VISUALIZE

PERSONALIZE

By faith I'll decide that I, because I'm a new creature, have no interest whatsoever in sinning. I'll consider myself ready to receive God's love, power, grace and resurrection life which are mine in Christ Jesus.

PRAY THE VERSE, APPLYING IT TO YOUR LIFE

Dear God, by faith I count myself dead to ______ (recurring sin). By faith I'll decide I'm alive to God and His power to ______ (do whatever is necessary in you to remove the temptation to sin again in this area). Thank you that I'm a new creature in Christ Jesus.

TRIUMPH OVER TEMPTATION

List the tantalizing attractions the devil usually parades in front of you. How can counting yourself dead to sin and alive to Jesus cause you to lose all interest in disobeying Him?

WEEK 6
DAY 1

Are You Planning to Wear Forgiveness Today?

Nicole stood in front of her closet door. Usually she put her heart into deciding what to wear so she could look just right. This morning she really didn't care. Randomly pulling out an orange blouse and a pink skirt, she jerked to her senses. She couldn't wear *that*, no matter how she felt.

Then her mind returned to the reason she had spent a sleepless night. She and Chad had been going together for over a year. Although Chad had been overcritical and she'd been supersensitive during the last two months, she never thought there was anything seriously wrong. She had always tried to be supportive when he told her how hard things were at home and had spent hours helping him with his homework. Coming to school and finding him at Nancy's locker took her by surprise. The fact that neither of them would even speak to her was the thing that hurt worst.

The least Chad could have done was explain his new feelings to her and thank her for all she'd done for him. Why didn't he tell her what was wrong? Why didn't he even want to be her friend?

Out of habit, Nicole sat down to read something out of the Bible before she went to school. A verse in Colossians caught her eye. "Dearly loved, clothe yourselves with compassion, kindness, humility, gentleness and patience.

Bear with each other and forgive whatever grievances you may have against one another. Forgive as the Lord forgave you" (Col. 3:12, 13).

She decided to read the whole chapter. The first part told her to get rid of anger because she'd taken off her old self and had put on her new self. She wondered how she could just take off anger, jealousy and resentment and put on gentleness, love and forgiveness. The Bible sounded as if it were just as easy as changing clothes, but her hurt feelings were screaming at her, telling her that Chad didn't even deserve to be forgiven.

Then she remembered two things. The first was a Bible verse she had learned: "The righteous will live by faith" (Rom. 1:17). The second was something she'd read in Hannah Whithall Smith's famous book, *The Christian's Secret of a Happy Life* about putting your will in the right place and letting your emotions come tagging along behind.

She realized that by faith she could *will* to forgive Chad and could put on love. She could go to school wearing gentleness and humility. She had already overruled her emotions once that day. Although she didn't care what she looked like (and even thought of looking her worst to gain some sympathy), her mind told her to wear something that looked nice. Her emotions weren't very happy, but they didn't get to rule.

In the same way, she could set her mind on forgiveness and ignore the emotional outcry to do something drastic to get Chad's attention, or to let self-pity drive her into deep depression. It was like standing at her closet door once more. The dresses were labeled "bitterness," "jealousy," "resentment," "anger"—and "forgiveness." By faith she chose forgiveness.

MEMORIZE

"Put off your old self, which is being corrupted by its deceitful desires; to be made new in the attitude of your minds; and to put on the new self, created to be like God in true righteousness and holiness" (Eph. 4:22–24).

VISUALIZE

PERSONALIZE

By faith I can take off my old reactions and through studying the Bible and spending time with God in prayer, my attitude will change so I'll be wearing my new self that does right things.

PRAY THE VERSE, APPLYING IT TO YOUR LIFE

Dear God, I know that ________ was the wrong thing to do. Please forgive me. Through your Word, change my mind-set. Thank you that I am a new creature and that I can let the new me show up on the outside.

PICK OUT A NEW WARDROBE

Label the outfits your flesh would like to wear today. Meditate on some Bible verses that tell you the right way to overcome these wrong attitudes. By faith, what will the new you choose to wear today?

WEEK 6
DAY 2

Do You Have Some Extra Faith in the Bank?

When Todd became a Christian, he stopped doing drugs. In many ways, he saw how powerful God really was. He believed that God would help him stay in school and become a better student, and his faith was rewarded. He believed that God could give him love for his family, and he experienced a miracle inside. Whenever he felt that depression which he used to alleviate with drugs, he read his Bible and used praise and thanksgiving as his weapons. It worked.

But when he added a job to his already busy schedule—and then came down with a bad case of the flu—he became very discouraged. He got into a heavy argument with his father and he felt that old hatred creeping back. Facing a week's make-up work, he wanted to drop out and forget it. The devil was right there to try to steal all his faith. The old thought pattern ("you'll-never-get-through-this-one-without-taking-some-more-drugs") came at him with such force he didn't think he'd be able to resist it. Then the devil came in for the kill: "Look, you don't have any faith left. You might as well stop even trying to be a Christian."

Have you ever been in the same situation as Todd? The devil always tries to destroy our faith because he, too, knows that "the righteous will live by faith" (Rom. 1:17). In order to make you sin, he must rob your faith. Your first line of defense is not using your willpower to resist temptation; it's guarding your faith and building it up by meditating on God's Word.

Col. 1:21, 22 puts it like this: "Once you were alienated from God and were enemies in your minds because of your evil behavior. But now he has reconciled you by Christ's physical body through death to present you holy in his sight, without blemish and free from accusation—*if you continue in your faith, established and firm, not moved from the hope held out in the gospel.*"

But you can't wait until you're sick and are bombarded with all kinds of trials and temptations to establish yourself in the faith. You must put something in your bank account *now* and save it for a rainy day. If truly respecting and loving your parents is a problem for you, memorize and internalize verses about honoring parents and loving people. In this way you'll build a strong wall against attack along these lines. If you have a tendency to quit when things get tough, arm yourself with scripture passages on perseverance and hard work. If you're often tempted to return to drugs and alcohol when you feel depressed, learn with the psalmist how to praise and thank your way out of those nasty moods.

In Jude, verse 20, we find this command: "Build yourself up in your most holy faith." Do you have some extra faith in the bank? You're going to need it. If you have nothing to fall back on, you can't replenish the faith the devil succeeds in stealing from you in a moment of weakness.

MEMORIZE

"Consequently, faith comes from hearing the message, and the message is heard through the word of Christ" (Rom. 10:17).

VISUALIZE

PERSONALIZE

I can build up my faith by listening to others teach the Bible and through reading and meditating on God's Word myself.

PRAY THE VERSE, APPLYING IT TO YOUR LIFE

Dear God, I need faith for ______. I ask you to put me in contact with someone who can teach me the biblical truths I need for this situation. Show me the verses that apply to my problem and I will meditate on them.

MEDITATE ON SCRIPTURE

Make a card like this one and take it with you today. In each spare moment reread the verse and let its truth change your life. Go to sleep thinking about this verse.

WEEK 6
DAY 3

Joseph, Moses, Paul—and Me?

Troy and Andy attended a workshop called "Teens Can Change the World." After school on Monday, they decided to witness to the kids who were watching the football team practice and to some who were hanging out at the local burger palace.

The first guy they tried to talk to laughed in their faces and called them religious fanatics. Then they talked to a whole group of indifferent students. The next guy said, "If God gives out free cocaine, I'll follow Him."

Tempted to become discouraged, they remembered what they had learned at the conference: "If the devil attacks you, persevere in faith until your seeming defeat turns into victory."

So they opened up more conversations and heard more kids put them down. A Jewish boy was especially angry at their attempt to try to convert him. Because it was soon suppertime, they prepared to leave. Just then, someone called out their names. Surprised, they turned around to see that Leon, the first guy they had talked to, was walking up to them.

"I know I laughed at you," he began. "But I've been following you around all afternoon. What is it that you guys have? How can you keep your cool and keep up your courage when everyone laughs in your face? Your promise to pray for me and showing me love is something I've never seen." And so that day, Leon accepted Jesus into his heart.

Has anything like that ever happened to you? Or are you a "I'm-an-outnumbered-Christian-in-a-big-bad-world-and-the-devil's-attacking-me-so-I-might-as-well-give-up" type? The Bible says (guess what!), "The righteous will live by faith" (Rom. 1:17). And part of that faith includes this verse: "Let us not become weary in doing good, for at the proper time we will reap a harvest if we do not give up" (Gal. 6:9).

It's relatively easy to have faith for a short period of time—or if everything seems to be going well. If you study the lives of men and women who did great things for God, however, you'll discover their secret. Although they were people just like you and me with hang-ups and problems, they learned to persevere in faith.

Moses did not go back to Egypt when the desert complainers tried his patience to the limit. Joseph didn't stop trusting God even though he experienced slavery and prison. Paul continued to preach despite stonings, beatings and shipwreck. And that's what you need as well—faith that lasts through trials, temptations and boredom.

When you realize that the main strategy of the devil is to arrange circumstances so that things appear hopeless, you can decide to walk by faith and not by sight. You can determine to keep on doing what is right and trusting God until you see the final victory. God can actually use all Satan's roadblocks to let you see more of His power. Without great battles, there are no great victories. But if you allow the devil to rob your faith, you'll think you're defeated and stop fighting. Instead, join Joseph, Moses, Paul and all the other overcomers.

MEMORIZE

"So, do not throw away your confidence; it will be richly rewarded. You need to persevere so that when you have done the will of God, you will receive what he has promised" (Heb. 10:35–36).

VISUALIZE

PERSONALIZE

I won't throw away the faith I have that God will act for me. God will reward my faith. I will hang on and do God's will. Then I'll see the fulfillment of God's promises.

PRAY THE VERSE, APPLYING IT TO YOUR LIFE

Dear God, I still believe you for ______ (problem that seems to be getting worse). I know that you will give me the answer if I keep on trusting in you. Show me if I am missing your will in anyway so I can qualify for all of your promises.

PUT ON A "BLESSED ARE ALL WHO WAIT FOR HIM" ATTITUDE SO YOU WON'T MISS OUT ON ONE OF GOD'S PROMISES

Write down the things that have been discouraging you lately. With a red pen, write over each one: "You need to persevere so that when you have done the will of God, you will receive what He has promised."

WEEK 6
DAY 4

Self-Examination

1. Saying, "I am righteous in Jesus," means
   _____ a. Jesus died to erase my sin, so I can do whatever I want without penalty.
   _____ b. God looks at me as righteous even though I'm still a dirty rotten sinner who has no hope of changing my bad habits.
   _____ c. I become righteous by faith and I stay righteous by faith—I can receive God's power for victory over sin.
   _____ d. None of the above.
2. I sin because
   _____ a. I have lack of faith.
   _____ b. I basically enjoy sinning.
   _____ c. I'm especially swayed by peer pressure.
   _____ d. The devil picks on me more than others.
3. My body, mind, emotions and will
   _____ a. Are no good because I'm only a sinner saved by grace.
   _____ b. Can easily get off track if I let them run wild.
   _____ c. Can be a real help to my obeying God if they are disciplined and put under the power of the Holy Spirit.
   _____ d. Are what the Bible refers to as my "flesh," which is not the deepest part of me and won't live forever.
4. "The righteous shall live by ________________."
   Reference ______________________________

5. What is your first line of defense against temptation?
   _____ a. Isolating yourself against non-Christians so you won't be tempted.
   _____ b. Doing so many good things that you have no time for bad things.
   _____ c. Keeping your faith strong and building it up by Scripture meditation.
   _____ d. Using your willpower to resist temptation.
6. How do you "put faith in the bank"?
   _____ a. Always be positive.
   _____ b. Daily meditate on Scripture.
   _____ c. Go to seminary.
   _____ d. Hang around people who have a lot of faith.
7. What problem will you face if you decide to live by faith?
   _____ a. The devil will try to steal your faith.
   _____ b. You'll be tempted to give up if the answer doesn't come within a reasonable period of time.
   _____ c. You'll have to ignore what you see and believe that God's Word is true regardless of circumstances.
   _____ d. All of the above.
8. Has anyone said anything negative about you lately? _____ How did you respond? _____ Did you ask God if the statement was true? _____ Did you find a Bible verse to meditate on that will help you make needed changes or that will keep you from false condemnation? _________
9. What was hard about the week? _________ Did you remember to ask God for some mercy, forgiveness, favor, kindness, (grace)? _________________
10. How has realizing that you're a new creature in Christ helped you this week? _________________

---

1. c. **2.** a. **3.** b. c. d. **4.** Faith, Rom. 1:17. **5.** c. **6.** b. **7.** d.
8.–10. Personal.

PART 4

In Jesus I Am Redeemed

In him we have redemption through his blood, the forgiveness of sins, in accordance with the riches of God's grace.

Ephesians 1:7

WEEK 6
DAY 5

It's All in a Word

Redemption is a word that might not be in your vocabulary. It should be. Its meaning may best be explained by an illustration.

General Smith had his strategy planned. The army engineers would destroy the bridge, thus preventing the enemy from crossing the river. At the same time they would launch a surprise artillery attack from the surrounding mountains and slowly close the trap. His intention was to force the entire division to surrender. Captain Carlson, however, was an hour late bringing his demolition crew to the bridge, resulting in the escape of every enemy soldier and the capture of himself and his men.

Losing this golden opportunity meant initiating peace negotiations. General Smith got nowhere in his effort to end the war and to liberate the prisoners. Finally, he said, "I'll be a P.O.W. so Captain Carlson and his men can go free!" Because the offer was accepted, Captain Carlson returned to his company and even got back his old position.

This story has the main elements of redemption: Rescuing or liberating someone by paying a great price and setting a person free from the penalties and guilt of wrong-doing.

In Jesus you have redemption. You have complete forgiveness for your sins. Jesus took your place on the cross and He went to hell for you. What a price He paid to rescue you! If you give your life to Jesus and accept His pardon, you won't get what you deserve—you'll go to heaven!

But that isn't all. God wants to redeem the things marred by sin's consequences. Sin caused the alcoholism or divorce that wrecked your family and adversely affected your personality: God wants to gently heal your wounds as He continually pours His love into them. Anger was behind the words that hurt you so much: God wants to teach you to forgive the guilty person and to erase those words with His own. He wants to restore the mind burned out by drugs and replace rebellion with self-discipline. He can even use your bad experiences and a past you're ashamed of to give you insights into other people and to demonstrate His power and glory.

"And we know that in all things God works for the good of those who love him, who have been called according to his purpose" (Rom. 8:28). It's all in a word. And that word is redemption.

WEEK 7
DAY 1

Eternal Redemption and Stopping at Red Lights

I once asked a student if he'd had a good weekend. "No," he replied. "It was terrible. I ran a red light and hit a police car. Besides, I was drunk and driving without a license!" To that student, the law was a real curse.

The Bible affirms, "Christ redeemed us from the curse of the law" (Gal. 3:13). Some people think this means that Christians can do whatever they wish since God has removed all the red lights from life. That simply isn't true. God gave His people, the Israelites, three kinds of law: ceremonies like Passover, which were acted-out prophecies pointing toward the coming of Christ; civil laws to govern the nation of Israel; and moral laws. The first two kinds of laws are no longer binding since Christ has already come and the theocracy (rule by God) of the ancient Israelites no longer exists. God's moral law, however, remains the same. The rules haven't changed, but the curse is gone.

A red light doesn't need to be a curse. It can be a real blessing! In fact, speed limits, one-way streets and yield signs were all designed for your safety and protection. It's only when you're paying the traffic ticket or viewing that crumpled front fender that you find the law unreasonable.

Jesus died, not to take away God's eternal standards, but the curse of the law. Although there was forgiveness in Old Testament times, the necessary, continual blood sacrifices were sickening reminders of the curse. Watching that beautiful innocent lamb become a matted mass of blood-drenched fleece gave the sinner a graphic reminder of the consequences of wrongdoing. Not only that, he knew the same scene would be repeated over and over again. But Jesus changed all that: "He did not enter by means of the blood of goats and calves; but he entered the Most Holy Place once for all by his own blood, *having obtained eternal redemption*" (Heb. 9:12). Jesus paid the price for your sin once and for all—you never need to enact another ceremony to be cleansed of it! If you confess and forsake your sin, He'll forgive you.

Jesus not only died, but He rose again as conqueror over Satan and sin. Both the forgiveness and the victory over sin can be yours because of Jesus' death. "The death he died, he died to sin once for all; but the life he lives, he lives to God. In the same way, count yourselves dead to sin but alive to God in Christ Jesus" (Rom. 6:10–11). In addition to taking advantage of His forgiveness when you fail, you need to realize that God has good reasons for all the commandments in the Bible and that He offers you supernatural power to obey them.

Stoplights are fine if you have good brakes, a heart full of God-given patience and a feeling that traffic signs are there to help you. In the same way, God's commandments are great if you trust God's wisdom in giving them, have asked forgiveness for breaking them, and are depending on the Jesus-power inside you for keeping them. Jesus, the curse-remover, wants you to have a new perspective on life. And that's what stopping at red lights has to do with eternal redemption.

MEMORIZE

Jesus Christ, "who gave himself for us to redeem us from all wickedness and to purify for himself a people that are his very own, eager to do what is good" (Titus 2:14).

VISUALIZE

PERSONALIZE

Jesus paid the price to rescue me from sin, making me pure. I'm His very own child and He's put the Holy Spirit inside of me to make me want to do good things like ______ .

PRAY THE VERSE, APPLYING IT TO YOUR LIFE

Dear God, thanks for sending Jesus to give His life a ransom for me. Thanks for making it possible for purity to take the place of sin in my life. You can give me victory over ______ (tough sin). Thank you that I'm yours and am eager to do what is right.

MEDITATE ON SCRIPTURE

Copy this card to take along with you today. Meditate on the verse and digest it. Keep the verse in mind as you go to sleep tonight.

WEEK 7
DAY 2

Faith—the Price Tag of a New Life

Peggy looked at her protruding tummy. She knew she wouldn't be able to hide the fact that she was pregnant much longer. Her mother was already suspicious. (She'd missed ten days of school this semester.) When her little brother commented at dinner that she was getting fat, she had burst into tears. Peggy viewed herself in the mirror, and in her mind's-eye she saw what she would look like four months later.

Why had she ruined her whole life? Why had she rebelled against her strict Christian parents to date Bill on the sly? Why had she believed him when he said he loved her and that sex was the only way they could truly express their love for each other? Why had he dropped her like a hot potato when she told him she was going to have a baby? Would God ever forgive her? Would she ever be happy again? She felt so alone and so scared. Not knowing which way to turn, she broke into sobs and buried her head in her pillow.

Maybe you, like Peggy, feel marked for life by the consequences of sin. Perhaps past wrongdoing continues to haunt you and you wonder if you'll ever be free from guilt. As you view the shambles of your existence, do you doubt your ability to become a success?

There is good news for you! For those who truly repent (not just feel sorry that what they did got them in trouble) and agree with God that their action is sin and determine to stop their wrongdoing, there is not only forgiveness but restoration—a new life.

A good example of what God can do with a person who has ruined his life, and perhaps the lives of others, is found in the Old Testament story of King Manasseh. He not only worshiped idols but sacrificed his sons to them and carried images of them into God's temple. He practiced witchcraft, led the people of Jerusalem into deeper wickedness than surrounding nations, and paid no attention when the Lord tried to speak to him. But as a P.O.W. in Assyria, he repented. God not only pardoned him, but gave him back his throne, used him to destroy all the idols and lead his people back to God.

No matter what you've done, you, like Manasseh, can return to God and receive his complete forgiveness and power to live a new life. God says to you, "I, even I, am he who blots out your transgressions, for my own sake, and remembers your sins no more" (Isa. 43:25). And there is the promise: "God made him who had no sin to be sin for us, so that in him we might become the righteousness of God" (2 Cor. 5:21). Because of Jesus' death, God can offer you a trade—your sin for His righteousness! It's the best deal in the world. The only price is faith. Like Manasseh, you can change from questioning and breaking God's rules to believing that He has good reasons for each command and supernatural power for you to obey. You can have faith that when He says He'll forgive you completely and give you an entirely new life, He will. When you face each moment knowing that a loving and all-powerful God is in control, there is no reason to sin. The price tag on that brand new life you need says "faith."

MEMORIZE

"For in the gospel a righteousness from God is revealed, a righteousness that is by faith from first to last, just as it is written: 'The righteous will live by faith' " (Rom. 1:17).

VISUALIZE

PERSONALIZE AND READ OUT LOUD

God's good news shows me how to live right. From beginning to end, actions that please God depend on my faith. I can read it in the Old Testament: Those who live right act in faith.

PRAY THE VERSE, APPLYING IT TO YOUR LIFE

Dear God, thank you that you've given me the secret for living your way. Thank you that as I trust that your rules are best for me and have faith that you have things under control, I can live right. Thanks, Lord, that if I live by faith I can live to please you.

PUT YOUR FAITH INTO PRACTICE

Check the items that apply to you and fill in the blanks.

____ 1. If I believe God can do anything, I'll stop worrying about ______________________________.

____ 2. If I receive God's love by faith, I can even love __________.

____ 3. If I believe God can fulfill my needs, I can break up with ________________ and stop hanging around with __________.

WEEK 7
DAY 3

And Then the Crash

Bernie was a new Christian, but he wasn't very happy. His mind kept flashing back to the one day in his B.C. life he just couldn't forget.

It was the last day of school and students had been dismissed at 11:30 a.m. Steve had invited the gang over for a couple cases of beer. Celebrating the end of school with abandon, Bernie drank a lot. "Let's go to McDonalds," someone suggested, and four friends hopped into his car.

Bernie was driving Indianapolis-500-style when suddenly a blond, four-year-old boy ran in front of the car. The boy was killed instantly.

That limp, blood-stained body, the hysterical cries of his mother, and the heartless questions of the policeman rushed across his mind as he relived the scene. And then came the words that lived to torture him: The mother had screamed, "You killed my boy!" Mentally, Bernie received his six-hundredth and eighty-ninth conviction for murder.

Six months after the accident, Bernie had accepted Jesus as his Savior. Although he knew his sins were forgiven and he could go to heaven, that cloud of guilt would not leave him. He was redeemed, but he didn't feel redeemed.

Do you identify with Bernie's problem? It might be

good for you to realize that Moses was a murderer, David was an adulterer and Paul a persecutor of Christians. God forgave each of these men and used them mightily. The reason God could re-tool their lives and make them into heroes of the faith is that they received God's pardon and lived like forgiven men.

Let God's Word sink deep into your spirit. "For as high as the heavens are above the earth, so great is his love for those who fear him; as far as the east is from the west, so far has he removed our transgressions from us. As a father has compassion on his children, so the Lord has compassion on those who fear him; for he knows how we are formed, he remembers that we are dust" (Ps. 103:11–14).

Who are you to argue with God and decide not to feel forgiven? Here are a couple verses you need to memorize. "For I will forgive their wickedness and will remember their sins no more" (Heb. 8:12). And, "You will again have compassion on us; you will tread our sins underfoot and hurl our iniquities into the depths of the sea" (Mic. 7:19). God forgot about your sin, and you should, too!

And one big crash (or mistake or set of circumstances) can't ruin your life, because there's such a thing as redemption—the restoration of ruined lives.

MEMORIZE

"Put your hope in the Lord, for with the Lord is unfailing love and with him is full redemption" (Ps. 130:7).

VISUALIZE

PERSONALIZE

I will trust in God. His love will never fail me. He will make something beautiful out of the tangled mess of my past.

PRAY THE VERSE, APPLYING IT TO YOUR LIFE

Dear God, thank you that I can put my faith in you and your unchanging love. Thank you that you will completely redeem each part of my life—scars and all.

ACCEPT GOD'S LOVE

Make a list of the things that have kept you from God's love. With a red pen, write over each one: "For with the Lord is unfailing love and with Him is full redemption."

WEEK 7
DAY 4

If You Blew It—There's a New It!

It was December 31, and as he thought back, Josh wished he could erase the entire year.

He had dropped out of school in March and had started hanging around with the wrong crowd. Twice caught shoplifting and once robbing McDonalds, he now had a police record and was on probation. His father's disapproval of him came out in a dozen ways. Fired from his job for coming late too often, he now faced going back to school, or getting kicked out of the house. Besides, Shelly had broken up with him and he missed her a lot.

Have you ever considered trying a way to wipe out part of your life? Although you don't peel away portions of your life the way you tear pages off a calendar, something can be done to make up for lost time. The Bible calls it redemption, or restoration. An interesting example is found in the Book of Joel.

In order to make residents of Judah return to the Lord, God permitted a drought and allowed grasshoppers to eat whatever crops came up. Joel, the prophet, called the people to repent and then gave them God's promise: "I will repay you for the years the locusts have eaten" (Joel 2:25). God is saying to you, "I want to repair the part of your life you've ruined."

It works like this: Josh could cooperate with God as he studied and end up graduating with honors. The couple who had to get married could completely repent and appropriate God's blessing for the home they establish. The boy who stole money can work and pay back more than he took. In addition, he can learn God's lesson of contentment so he'll be satisfied with what he had and never be tempted to steal again. God can give *you* the guts to tell the geometry teacher that you've cheated your way through the semester and deserve to fail. You could permit God to restore, not only your clear conscience, but confidence in your ability to do math. Then God can use these bad experiences in your life both to teach you things and to help you share with others.

One of the devil's chief lies is, "Now you've blown everything and there's no hope for you." Don't let him pull one over on you. Hang on to some of the promises in the Bible: "For his anger lasts only a moment, but his favor lasts a lifetime; weeping may remain for a night, but rejoicing comes in the morning" (Ps. 30:5). "I will build you up again and you will be rebuilt" (Jer. 31:4). "Instead of their shame my people will receive a double portion, and instead of disgrace they will rejoice in their inheritance" (Isa. 61:7). Quote these verses to the devil if you have to, but whatever you do, believe the Bible instead of Satan's lies.

God sent Jeremiah down to the potter's house to learn about redemption. As the potter worked the clay, he came up with a defective vase, but he didn't throw it away—he just made it over again. Your hardness may have produced some very ugly spots, but God is the Master Potter who wants to rework that clay into something beautiful if you yield your life to Him. Because of God's compassion and power, if you blew it there's still a *new* it!

MEMORIZE

"Then you will know that I, the Lord, am your Savior, your Redeemer, the Mighty One of Jacob. Instead of bronze I will bring you gold, and silver in place of iron" (Isa. 60:16–17).

VISUALIZE

PERSONALIZE

I know that you're the One who saves me and rescues me. You've got something better for me than what I'm experiencing right now.

PRAY THE VERSE, APPLYING IT TO YOUR LIFE

Dear God, thanks for always being ready to save and deliver me. Instead of _______ (problem in some area of life), you will give me victory. Instead of _______ (difficult emotion), you will bring me peace.

LET JESUS REMODEL YOUR HEART-HOUSE

Imagine Jesus as the repairman who has just come to your heart-house to do some remodeling. In order to replace the bronze with gold, there are some things you must part with. Ask Jesus what you need to give up to Him so He can remake you.

WEEK 7
DAY 5

Boredom Blasted by Blessings

Kirk sighed as his physics teacher launched into his "When-I-was-in-high-school-students-respected-their-teachers" speech. Kirk had heard it so many times he could have given it himself.

His next class was social problems, in which speeches on the dangers of nuclear war resulted in his having to hear basically the same information thirty times. And the finale of his schoolday was language lab, in which the most exciting thing that could occur was getting to repeat a *new* French phrase over and over again.

Having worked at Burger King three years, Kirk also longed for a more challenging job—he couldn't stand the thought of eating another hamburger. Even the church youth group seemed boring—always singing the same songs and endlessly discussing whether or not Christians should go to movies, watch certain TV programs, or listen to rock music.

Kirk knew Jesus had saved him from sin, but deep in his heart he wanted more.

One day as he opened his Bible, a verse literally jumped out at him. It read: "With joy you will draw water from the wells of salvation" (Isa. 12:3). It dawned on him: "Salvation is more than fire insurance to keep me out of hell. It has something to offer me right now."

Col. 1:13–14 confirmed that new revelation: "For he

has rescued us from the dominion of darkness and brought us into the kingdom of the Son he loves in whom we have redemption, the forgiveness of sins." This really meant that the price had already been paid, not only to forgive his sins, but to bring him into another dimension of living. He'd heard about "kingdom kids" before, but now he realized what it meant: God's inexhaustible supply of power is there to save us from anything the devil has planned to make our lives miserable. He really could draw waters from the wells of salvation with the assurance that God wanted to do something about his lackluster life!

Like Kirk, you may never have realized the extent of God's redemption. The word *salvation* in Isa. 12:3 means "aid, victory, prosperity, deliverance, health, help, save, welfare"—and that covers a lot of territory. You can ask God to save you from boredom, loneliness, depression, sickness and confusion. Whatever your problem, God *wants* to deliver you with *His solution*.

Because people tell God how to rescue them and give Him their timetable, they "lose their faith," thinking God did not answer. Your part is to put your faith in Jesus as your Savior and Redeemer from the present problem and to claim the deliverance God has promised. Maybe you, like Kirk, need to hold on in faith until the headlines of your life read: "Boredom Blasted by Blessings!"

MEMORIZE

"For you know that it was not with perishable things such as silver or gold that you were redeemed from the empty way of life handed down to you from your forefathers, but with the precious blood of Christ" (1 Pet. 1:18–19).

VISUALIZE

PERSONALIZE

I know that the price to rescue me from the meaningless life of this world was paid by the precious blood of Jesus, which is more costly than silver or gold.

PRAY THE VERSE, APPLYING IT TO YOUR LIFE

Dear God, thank you for sending Jesus to deliver me from ______ (vicious circle in your life) with the price of His blood.

MEDITATE ON SCRIPTURE

Make a copy of this card and take it with you today. Use each spare moment to meditate on the verse. As you drift off to dreamland tonight, think about this verse.

WEEK 8
DAY 1

Vaporizing Vicious Circles

Heather stopped for a minute as she surveyed her disorderly room.

Dirty clothes filled one corner. Her dresser was stacked high with textbooks, scattered pages of a term paper she was working on, and half the cassettes she owned. On her vanity were enough bottles and jars to stock the health and beauty department at K-Mart. Dreading what she might find under the bed, Heather tried to mentally change the subject. But her mother's angry words about having a disobedient daughter who couldn't even honor her mother by keeping a neat room filled her eyes with tears. Why couldn't she be like her mother—automatically tidy?

Heather remembered a Sunday school lesson on redemption in which her teacher stated that God wanted to restore weak and broken parts of each person's personality. Heather knew that if God said she was redeemed from futile ways, it was true. But she certainly didn't *feel* redeemed. She also knew that the Bible taught children to obey their parents. But if she were totally honest, keeping a clean room (or even straightening it up in the first place) seemed like an utter impossibility. Why couldn't she be different, or why couldn't her mother understand that she wasn't purposely trying to be rebellious? How could she receive God's redemption for the situation?

Heather recalled what she had read in her Bible the day before: "When they . . . compare themselves with themselves, they are not wise" (2 Cor. 10:12). She couldn't compare herself with her mother. She had to be able to accept herself with her weaknesses just as God did. Another verse came to her mind: "And everything that does not come from faith is sin" (Rom. 14:23). Suddenly she realized the root of her problem—she considered herself hopeless, she thought of cleaning her room as an impossibility and she presumed that not even God could change her mother's utter disgust for the slightest bit of messiness. The Bible called her lack of faith sin, and she had to confess it as such.

Although Heather knew it would be uphill all the way, she could see that nobody was ever redeemed without faith. People even miss heaven because of lack of faith. And she couldn't take advantage of God's power to restore and renovate areas of her life without stick-to-it faith and action based on firm trust in God. Heather also saw how the devil continually tried to cause her to put her mind on all the past failures in this area to snuff out any faith that might be rising within her. She determined to believe that God could rectify the situation and to pray for specific changes.

She discovered that her hurt feelings from constantly being compared with her neat and organized sister had caused her to judge her mother. She reasoned, "If my mother is such a good Christian, she should accept me even if I am disorganized." Because she anticipated her mother's predictable criticism of her feeble attempts to clean up her room, her heart had become hardened and she didn't even try anymore.

Heather read Ps. 25:9: "He guides the humble in what is right and teaches them his way." She acknowledged the pride of thinking she knew where the first change had to come. Heather resolved to ask God to soften her heart and to give her the next step, and the next and the next. She thought, "God really does have a way of vaporizing vicious circles." Then she lifted up her bedspread and started putting away the things she found under her bed.

MEMORIZE

"You are my hiding place; you will protect me from trouble and surround me with songs of deliverance" (Ps. 32:7).

VISUALIZE

PERSONALIZE

God is my security when I feel like I'm under attack. He will protect me from my own foolishness and from undeserved criticism. He'll deliver me and give me a song in my heart.

PRAY THE VERSE, APPLYING IT TO YOUR LIFE

Dear God, thank you that I can come to you today and find refuge from _______ (problem you have). Protect me from _______ (attack on your life) and surround me with joy and freedom to tackle _______ (a job you must do but are afraid of).

EXPERIENCE SONGS OF DELIVERANCE!

Ask God to protect you from trouble and surround you with songs of deliverance all day long. Cooperate with Him by singing songs of praise whenever you have the opportunity.

WEEK 8
DAY 2

What You **Receive** Is What You Get

There's a movie version of the old book, *Pilgrim's Progress*. The main character, Pilgrim, goes from place to place carrying a heavy burden and trying to find peace. Finally he comes to the foot of the cross where he sees Jesus suffering and paying the price of his freedom. Realizing that Jesus purchased his liberty, he drops the burden and walks on in joy and victory.

The story of Pilgrim is that of every true Christian—only sometimes we forget the cost and the meaning of redemption. And pick up our burden again.

Viewing the same scene from the viewpoint of heaven might help you capture its complete impact. In the Book of Revelation the Apostle John records seeing Jesus as the Lamb. This is the song those gathered around His throne sang: "You are worthy to take the scroll and to open its seals, because you were slain, and with your blood you purchased men for God from every tribe and language and people and nation. You have made them to be a kingdom and priests to serve our God, and they will reign on the earth" (Rev. 5:9–10).

If you capture what being redeemed (purchased for God by the blood of Jesus) really means, your life will never be the same again. Just try to take it all in:

- You are so important to God that He paid the price of your forgiveness with the blood of His only Son.

- You are part of God's redeemed family and have brothers and sisters all over the world.
- You are redeemed for the wonderful purpose of serving God on earth—doing work which has eternal value. "But you are a chosen people, a royal priesthood, a holy nation, a people belonging to God, that you may declare the praise of him who called you out of darkness into his wonderful light" (1 Pet. 2:9).
- You were bought by the blood of Jesus so you can have victory over the power of darkness and reign on earth right now.[1] "How much more will those who receive God's abundant provision of grace and of the gift of righteousness reign in life through one man, Jesus Christ" (Rom. 5:17). You can live above the problems the world tries to throw at you.

It's just that everyone else seems to be carrying a burden and the devil in all his subtlety tries to trip you into thinking it's your duty to pick it up. Or he just throws it on you when you're not looking and tries to convince you that it's not worth the struggle to get free of it again.

But Jesus rescued you from what disobedience brought to Adam and Eve—bondage to sin and life without meaning. In its place are forgiveness, hope of heaven and an important position in advancing His kingdom. Jesus successfully accomplished His rescue mission and offers you total freedom. What you *receive* is what you get.

---

[1]F. Davidson, A.M. Stibbs, and E.F. Kevan, eds., *The New Bible Commentary* (Grand Rapids: Eerdmans, 1960) p. 1177. "The RV follows the harder and therefore more likely reading in the second half of verse 10—"they reign [not shall reign] on earth."

MEMORIZE

"You were bought with a price. Therefore honor God in your body" (1 Cor. 6:20).

VISUALIZE

PERSONALIZE

It cost God the blood of Jesus to buy me. He bought me for the purpose of bringing praise to Him. He rescued me from the power of sin so I both want to and am able to honor God with my body.

PRAY THE VERSE, APPLYING IT TO YOUR LIFE

Dear God, thank you for loving me enough to pay such a high price for me. God, I want my lips to honor you today by ______, my hands to honor you today by ______, and my feet to honor you today by ______.

RECOGNIZE YOUR WORTH

Just sit still and ask God to show you how precious and valuable you are to Him. Realize what a privilege it is to bring honor to God by your life. You're an important part of the most wonderful venture in all the world—extending God's kingdom on earth.

WEEK 8
DAY 3

Self-Examination

1. Did you use the gift of righteousness to overcome any temptation this week? ____ Tell about it. ________
____
2. Did you "put some faith in the bank"? ____ Which verses did you make part of your life? ________
____
3. Did you accept God's kindness and favor to help you through any problems? ________________
Did you receive any rebuke that showed God's care for you in warning you of the consequences of following a wrong attitude or action? ____________
How are you going to change? ____________
____
Did you find any verses to help you? ________
List them. ____________________________
4. What does being a new creature in Christ mean to you? Complete a short paragraph. Because I am a new creature in Christ, ________________
____
____
5. What two concepts are included in redemption?
____
____
6. Being redeemed from the curse of the law means
____ a. I don't have to obey any command in the Old Testament.

____ b. I can now see that God's commands are there to help me. I have asked forgiveness for breaking them and am depending on Jesus' power in me for keeping them.

____ c. I should try hard to obey every command in the Bible knowing that I'll usually fail because I'm weak and sinful.

____ d. Since I'm not under law but under grace, I can view New Testament teachings as nice suggestions concerning my conduct.

7. I failed God but He wants to forgive me and redeem whatever I messed up. T F
8. I failed God so there's no hope for me. T F
9. One area of my life that I want God to redeem is ________________________________.

   (Pray daily for God to give you the first step in cooperating with Him, and put appropriate scriptures into your heart.)
10. How can studying about God's plan to redeem you give you a great sense of worth? ________________________________

1.–4. Personal. **5.** Rescuing or liberating someone by paying a great price and setting a person free from penalties and guilt or wrongdoing. **6.** b. **7.** T. **8.** F. **9.–10.** Personal.

PART 5

In Jesus I Am Accepted

Christ accepted you in order to bring praise to God.

Romans 15:7

WEEK 8
DAY 4

Not Even a Repair Bill

It was a cold November day. The gloomy sky matched the gray color of the streets below and that of the inner-city apartment complex where Joe lived. It began to rain and Joe shivered as he stopped to zip up his jacket. The drab surroundings highlighted the emptiness he felt inside—life without color, without meaning and without hope.

Joe thought of his family. His parents had split up, each to live with a different partner. Now he felt like an unwanted nuisance, with no place he could really call home. His teachers had always considered him a "disruptive influence," and he had spent more than his share of time in the assistant principal's office. A loner, he'd always had a hard time making friends. To top it off, Melissa, the only girl he had ever really cared about, had just said, "I'm sorry but I've found someone else who doesn't have so many problems and hang-ups."

Joe felt as if he had been rejected by everyone on earth. Living didn't seem worth the effort and he was seventeen.

Maybe you feel a lot like Joe. Perhaps you don't really sense acceptance by your parents. It could be that your older brother is a hard act to follow, that your personality is very different from your father's, or that they persecute you for following Jesus. Possibly school isn't easy for you and you're tired of seeing *C's* and *D's* on your papers. You may wonder why teachers seem to like A-students better than kids like you. It might be that your friends have disappointed you and you'd like to know where to go for acceptance.

A leper in the New Testament felt like that. Victim of an incurable and highly contagious disease, he was completely ostracized from society. Separated forever from family and friends, he couldn't count on anyone to fix him a meal, to wash his clothes, or invite him home for the evening. He lived a lonely, hopeless life.

But then the leper heard about the miracles of Jesus and determined to go to Him for help. When he saw Jesus, he got down on his knees and begged, "If you are willing, you can make me clean" (Mark 1:40).

"Filled with compassion, Jesus reached out his hand and touched the man" (Mark 1:41).

Imagine experiencing the loving touch of Jesus after such a long period of loneliness and rejection! Jesus cared about *him*. Jesus accepted *him*!

Jesus healed him as well. Jesus accepts you and loves you just as you are. But after He extends His hand of acceptance, He says, "I am willing"—to heal the hurt, to forgive the sin, and to remake your life.

You might be able to find another person who will love you just the way you are, but Jesus can do more. He can repair the damage and make you new. And He won't even send you a bill!

WEEK 8
DAY 5

"Just Accept Me—Don't Try to Change Me"

The shadows had begun to lengthen as the pale winter sun sank lower in the sky. The thermometer hovered near freezing, and the slopes were beginning to get icy. Having skied hard all day, Bob was exhausted. But when Scott yelled at him from the chair lift, "Meet you at the top and we'll race down," Bob couldn't say no.

A competitor at heart, Bob gave it all he had—but instead of turning neatly at the pole, he hit ice and veered out of control into the trees on the side of the mountain. Suddenly a stately Norwegian pine stopped him, and he felt excruciating pain in his right leg.

Vaguely, he recalled members of the ski patrol putting him on a sled, more pain, and a long ambulance ride to the hospital emergency room. Scott filled out the hospital form for him and a doctor in a white coat approached him. "Bob, I'm really glad to see you. I want you to know that I love you and accept you just the way you are. Don't be embarrassed about skiing into a tree and breaking your leg. It happens to the best of them. Here, there is nothing but total acceptance." And then he left the room.

Does this sound weird to you? Because the doctor had the capacity to change the situation for the better, we expect more than acceptance from him. To a much greater degree than any doctor, God has the power not only to accept you, but to change you. God's acceptance of you includes not only love, mercy and forgiveness, but surgery to remove that hatred, stitches to mend that broken heart, and out-patient therapy to teach you patience. *God completely accepts you in order to change you!*

This fact is often confusing. Since other people can't truly change us, we often resent their attempts. Most correction we receive from people is not really intended to help us, but to eliminate behavior they find bothersome. Our bosses nag us about laziness because they want the present task completed quickly. The teacher lectures about illegible handwriting and take points off for bad penmanship only after she's had a particularly bad week. Whether it's true or not, we hear the words, "It's all your fault." Because so many people reprimand us out of selfish motives, we tend to equate correction with lack of acceptance.

As we read the Bible and realize that we aren't living just as God intended, we often feel rejected by God, too. But God, like a good doctor, lovingly accepts his patients just as they are, while using His power to transform them. God accepts you and understands you totally. He just doesn't want you to go through life handicapped by a quick temper, a feeling of resentment, or a bad conscience. God accepts you just as you are; God wants to change you. Both statements are equally true.

Don't ever tell God, "Accept me but don't try to change me." Receive the acceptance of Jesus, and then let Him completely transform you.

MEMORIZE

"He has sent me to bind up the brokenhearted, to proclaim freedom for the captives . . . to comfort all who mourn . . . to bestow on them a crown of beauty instead of ashes" (Isa. 61:1–3).

VISUALIZE

PERSONALIZE

God sent Jesus to heal my heartache, to free me from my hang-ups, and to comfort me when I cry and to make the ugly things in my life into something beautiful.

PRAY THE VERSE, APPLYING IT TO YOUR LIFE

Dear God, thank you for sending Jesus to heal the deep hurt caused by ________ (something that causes pain whenever you think of it) and to free me from ________ (hang-up) that has been a prison for me. Thank you for comfort when I feel like crying. Lord, you know that ________ is a difficult situation. I ask you to resolve it and transform it into something good.

PERMIT JESUS TO MEND YOUR BROKEN HEART

Quietly sit in the presence of Jesus *receiving* inner healing, freedom from guilt and pressure, comfort, and renewal. Let the love and mercy of Jesus fill all the emptiness and erase all the hurt.

WEEK 9
DAY 1

At the Plate, Batting .000 We Have . . . a Future Babe Ruth!

It was spring in Chicago, and students had trouble keeping their minds on things like quotations from Macbeth, the structure of the human eye, and the functions of the three branches of the U.S. Government. Restless pupils looked out the windows and watched the clock as they thought about skipping school. In their daydreams, they were sipping chocolate milkshakes at the Dairy Queen, enjoying picnics in the country, boating on Lake Michigan and motorcycle racing.

For Wayne, spring brought one tremendous trial. The P.E. department chairman would always post baseball team assignments for the annual tournament. This year he had proudly announced that members of the winning team would get out of school to go see the Chicago Cubs. Skinny, uncoordinated, and the *worst* player on any team, Wayne considered the ordeal pure torture.

Feeling that the team was bound to lose because of him, he became so nervous he could hardly hold the bat, to say nothing about hitting the ball. He winced as the guys tried to put their strongest fielder in right and find a good shortstop to cover for his fumbles as third baseman. He'd been yelled at by so many gym teachers and teammates that he felt like wearing protective earplugs!

But the nightmare was on. The game had started and Wayne was up to bat. He tensed up and swung at a wild pitch.

Just then the new gym teacher called time out and took him aside. He put his hand on Wayne's shoulder. "Wayne," he said, "you'll do fine when you learn how to relax. Please come after school so I can work with you." Even that little encouragement helped and Wayne drew a walk.

After several sessions with the new gym teacher—the first gym teacher who had ever liked him!—his confidence began to grow and his nervousness to diminish. He even got a base hit.

There's something to learn from Wayne's experience. It was a wise person who said, "Accept me as I am so I may learn what I can become." What the gym teacher did for Wayne in the area of baseball, God wants to accomplish in your life. He accepts you as you are so through His power you can become something better. He told the woman caught in adultery, "Neither do I condemn you. Go now and leave your life of sin" (John 8:11). After Peter denied the Son of God, Jesus told him where to catch a lot of fish, made breakfast for him, and then entrusted him with giving God's Word to others. When Zachaeus was up a tree, Jesus found him, honored him by being his guest, and brought salvation tc his home.

This is what the Gospel is all about—the total acceptance and love of God for *you right now*, just as you are, so that He can make something beautiful out of your life.

Jesus saw in a prostitute a new woman of purity and worth, in a cowardly fisherman a dynamic preacher, and in a despised tax collector a man of generosity and compassion. The neat thing about Jesus is that you don't have to change to be accepted by Him. He takes you the way you are, and as you cooperate with Him, transforms you into someone who acts more and more like himself.

Even if your batting average is .000, Jesus looks at you and sees a future champion.

MEMORIZE

"But for that very reason I was shown mercy so that in me, the worst of sinners, Christ Jesus might display his unlimited patience as an example for those who would believe on him and receive eternal life" (1 Tim. 1:16).

VISUALIZE

PERSONALIZE

God wants to demonstrate His compassion to me and show off His unlimited patience to help me overcome _______ (tough-to-get-rid-of sin) so my life can be an example to others.

PRAY THE VERSE, APPLYING IT TO YOUR LIFE

Thank you, God, for your mercy and unlimited patience in my life. I want to cooperate with you so others can see big changes in my life.

JOIN YOUR PATIENCE WITH GOD'S

Side with God in accepting yourself as you are and *patiently* cooperating with Him for changes in your life. Thank God for His unlimited patience and mercy. Determine not to let your illusions or your impatience hinder you from cooperating as God changes you.

WEEK 9
DAY 2

Compare and . . . Crash!

Jody was discouraged. Although she was very thankful that she had invited Jesus into her heart, her Christian life was a struggle. She constantly compared herself to the other kids in her church. Most of them came from Christian homes and didn't swear, had never taken any drugs, and didn't even know the names of the songs she had constantly listened to. It seemed to her that they hardly had any temptations to resist.

Because her best friend, Carol, was always witnessing to kids at school and Jody was too timid to even open her mouth, she felt condemned and defeated. Why couldn't she just turn into Super Christian and be done with it? She felt that Jesus must be disappointed in her.

But one day as she was reading the Bible, she discovered something really neat, a passage in the Old Testament describing the character of Jesus: "A bruised reed he will not break, and a smoldering wick he will not snuff out. In faithfulness he will bring forth justice" (Isa. 42:3).

Instead of being "a shining light for Jesus," Jody identified more with that smoldering wick. Now she saw that Jesus came to earth to help weak people just like herself. She remembered Jesus' love for Peter, who denied Him, His compassion for the sick, and His forgiveness for the soldiers who nailed Him to the cross. Jesus accepted each person completely—strong or weak, rich or poor, lepers and small children, basket case or act-together-dude, Jew or Gentile. At that moment Jody realized that Jesus accepted her too—just the way she was.

Maybe you, like Jody, constantly compare yourself with other Christians. Perhaps you permit the Rules and Regulations Regiment in your church or the self-appointed members of the Criticism Committee to get to you. Possibly you've been deeply hurt by accusations that aren't true. Confess and forsake your sin, but don't try to please all the fans in the grandstand. (Popularity ratings don't give a sense of security and acceptance.) Take lessons from the Apostle Paul who said, "Now it is required that those who have been given a trust must prove faithful. I care very little if I am judged by you or by any human court; indeed, I do not even judge myself. My conscience is clear, but that does not make me innocent. *It is the Lord who judges me*" (1 Cor. 4:2–4).

Comparing yourself to others will lead to depression or pride. Paul warned people against it: "When they measure themselves by themselves and compare themselves with themselves; they are not wise" (2 Cor. 10:12). Let God be your judge, knowing that "all his ways are just" (Deut. 32:4). Remember that God grades on faithfulness, not on outward success.

How good to know that God accepts you and judges you fairly. He knows *all* the facts and understands your motives. So don't compare and crash. Enjoy being accepted by God and being fairly evaluated by the One who understands you completely.

MEMORIZE

"As a father has compassion on his children, so the Lord has compassion on those who fear him" (Ps. 103:13).

VISUALIZE

PERSONALIZE

Just like a father feels tenderness for his child, so God has mercy on me because I respect Him and intend to obey Him.

PRAY THE VERSE, APPLYING IT TO YOUR LIFE

Thank you, God, that your love and compassion toward me is like that of a father for his dear child. Thank you that your heart is open to me because I aim to pay attention to your words and to do as you say.

MEDITATE ON SCRIPTURE

Take a card like this with you today. Think about this verse during the natural breaks in your day. Go to sleep meditating on this verse.

WEEK 9
DAY 3

Somebody Believes in You

In 1929, Roy Riegals, a University of California football player who was much too nervous to be playing in the Rose Bowl, picked up a Georgia Tech fumble and headed for the end zone—in the wrong direction! A teammate, Benny Lom, chased him for sixty-five yards and tackled him just before he entered the wrong end zone.

Riegal's coach did not read him the riot act during halftime. He only announced that there would be no changes in the line-up. When Roy Riegals protested, explaining that he just couldn't face the crowd after having made such a terrible mistake, the coach encouraged him and sent him back to play again. That coach showed acceptance and demonstrated that he believed in Roy Riegals—no matter what.

God is like that coach. He has confidence in His children. This fact is portrayed in a story someone once wrote. It goes like this:

When Jesus returned to heaven after dying on the cross, He was asked by an angel, "What plan do you have for evangelizing the world?"

Jesus replied, "I chose twelve men to begin telling people around them. Those who believe their message will spread the good news to others until the whole world knows."

"And what if they fail?" the angel inquired.

Jesus replied: "I have no other plan."

Not only does God show His confidence in us by entrusting us with the Great Commission, the responsibility to tell the world about the new life available in Jesus, but He forgets about the sins and errors we confess to Him. Just read Hebrews 11, the Faith Hall of Fame chapter. God doesn't even mention the unbelief of Abraham and Sarah, the instability of Jacob, the murder that Moses committed, or the complaints of the Israelites. God chose to record the final results—the victories and not the blunders that were part of the struggle.

Maybe you wish that someone would believe in you instead of constantly pointing out your faults. You may long for a second chance to prove yourself in the eyes of a person who has already labeled you a failure. Perhaps you've said, "I just wish someone would accept me for what I am." God is that Person. Not only does He believe in you, but He offers you the unlimited power of the Holy Spirit—supernatural energy—so that the potential He sees in you can become a reality.

God chose you and entrusted you with His work. And like the University of California coach, God doesn't give up on you when you fumble, or if you carry the ball in the wrong direction. Somebody believes in you. And that Somebody is God.

MEMORIZE

"You did not choose me, but I chose you to go and bear fruit—fruit that will last. Then the Father will give you whatever you ask in my name" (John 15:16).

VISUALIZE

PERSONALIZE

I am accepted because Jesus specifically chose me to be productive spiritually—to accomplish things that will last through eternity. When heavenly values become important to me, God will give me whatever I ask for in Jesus' name.

PRAY THE VERSE, APPLYING IT TO YOUR LIFE

Dear God, thank you for choosing me. Thank you for entrusting to me the work of showing people by my life and witness that eternity can be different for them. Thank you, God, that when my mind is on eternal values you will give me whatever I ask in Jesus' name.

CELEBRATE THE FACT THAT YOU'VE BEEN PICKED FOR GOD'S TEAM

Walk around all day thinking, "I'm special because God chose me to do His work. I've been selected for the greatest honor on earth."

WEEK 9
DAY 4

A Special Place for You

Cindi always seemed to feel out of place.

Because she was shy and not very studious, she gave a sigh of relief when each class ended. She dreaded the thought of having to try to explain photosynthesis or being asked to list the causes of the Spanish-American War. Pop quizzes, chapter tests, oral reports and geometry homework seemed to chime in unison, "You're not quite with it, Cindi. The other kids know more than you do."

Never knowing quite what to say, she found social situations awkward. She always seemed to be on the fringe of the group of girls she tried to hang around with. Janet hadn't even invited her to the slumber party.

Although she knew her mother loved her, Cindi's stepfather had never really accepted her. When they had arguments centering around her, Cindi wished she could run away and find some place where she really belonged.

Do you identify with some of Cindi's feelings? Well, if you've received Jesus as your Savior and have given your whole life to Him, you've found your niche—you're a full-fledged member of the family of God. John 1:12 assures us: "Yet to all who received him, to those who believed in his name, he gave the right to become children of God." As a child of God, you'll *always* be loved and cared for because God has said, "Never will I leave you; never will I forsake you" (Heb. 13:5).

God loves all His children equally—no matter what they do or don't do. "Neither death nor life, neither angels nor demons, neither the present nor the future, nor any powers, neither height nor depth, nor anything else in all creation will be able to separate us from the love of God that is in Christ Jesus our Lord" (Rom. 8:39). Not only that, God has a wonderful inheritance for you—and He'll give you just as much as He gives to Jesus! "Now if we are children, then we are heirs—heirs of God and co-heirs with Christ" (Rom. 8:17). Jesus loves you so much that He is making a special place for you in heaven because He wants you to be with Him forever. He said, "I am going there to prepare a place for you. And if I go and prepare a place for you, I will come back and take you to be with me that you also may be where I am" (John 14:2–3).

God is saying, "You belong to me and I love you so much I'm making plans for you to live with me forever."

You also belong to God's family on earth—you have many brothers and sisters in Christ all over the world. "For we were all baptized by one Spirit into one body—whether Jews or Greeks, slaves or free—and we were all given the one Spirit to drink" (1 Cor. 12:13). Granted, many of God's children have a lot to learn about loving and accepting other people, but there is a bond among Christians that is even deeper than natural family ties. As Christians, we're secure in the love that Jesus has for us so we're free to really love each other. Because of Jesus, we're all part of God's family—and there's a special place in that family just for you.

MEMORIZE

"Since you are precious and honored in my sight and because I love you . . . Do not be afraid, for I am with you" (Isa. 43:4–5).

VISUALIZE

PERSONALIZE

I am important and valuable to God and He loves me. I don't need to be scared, because God is always with me.

PRAY THE VERSE, APPLYING IT TO YOUR LIFE

Dear God, how wonderful that I'm precious and important to you even though I sometimes feel ___________ (insecurity you face). Thank you for loving me and being with me always so I don't have to be afraid of ________ .

MEDITATE ON SCRIPTURE

Make your card to take with you today. Meditate on the verse and whenever you have two or three or more minutes to think apply it to your life. Go to sleep with this verse running through your mind.

WEEK 9
DAY 5

Are You One of God's Pets?

Jeff had to admit it. He was jealous of Brett and even went out of his way to point out Brett's faults.

It just didn't seem fair. Athletic and good-looking, Brett was a natural leader. In contrast, Jeff considered himself clumsy, ugly, and painfully shy. Brett got straight *A*'s, but Jeff had to work to come up with *B*'s and *C*'s. Brett's parents were Christians who loved each other, while Jeff's family was a mess. He hadn't even seen his father since he abandoned the family seven years before. His mother's boyfriend had just moved in, causing complete chaos. It seemed to Jeff that Brett must be God's pet and that God must have something against him.

Do you measure acceptance by the wrong yardstick? Do you feel that what God gave you in the first place—the raw material of your life, so to speak—is the final indicator of how He feels about you? (If so, God's acceptance is limited to a few pets born into favorable circumstances.) Or have you come to realize that consequences for sin and the demonstration of God's power to change circumstances and people are also principles built into the universe? Do you see that God's acceptance of you has to do with the process of turning out a finished product? Sometimes we forget that not all art masterpieces are made out of the same substance. It's the genius of the designer that produces greatness.

God's grace, love and approval are equally available to everyone. "The Lord delights in those who fear him, who put their hope in his unfailing love" (Ps. 147:11). The Lord does not delight only in certain "pets" to whom He gives all the breaks. When you reverence God and hope in His unfailing love, you can receive from Him all the acceptance and power you need to be a success for God. Some of the biggest treasures in His kingdom were made from "least-likely-to-succeed" people. It's not how you start out, but how you end up that counts.

So Jeff needs to look at himself and Brett from God's perspective. The same love, joy, peace and power is available to both of them. Brett could decide he could make it on his own and ruin his life, while Jeff could keep receiving from God and become a man mightily used by Him.

It's a well-known fact that Easy Street frequently produces spoiled brats and maladjusted adults. Because of this, God chose to allow obstacles and trials in His world. Rather than removing them, He provides us with power to overcome them. Anyone can tap into that power source. You're not God's pet—you don't need to be. God's got plenty of love, grace, time, encouragement and acceptance to give to all His children all the time.

MEMORIZE

"For the eyes of the Lord range throughout the earth to strengthen those whose hearts are fully committed to him" (2 Chron. 16:9).

VISUALIZE

PERSONALIZE

God looks down from heaven especially to strengthen me when my heart is totally dedicated to Him.

PRAY THE VERSE, APPLYING IT TO YOUR LIFE

Thank you, God, for looking out for me. Thank you that the people who are special to you and receive your strength are those whose hearts are fully committed to you. That means I can qualify.

BUILD YOUR DEFENSE AGAINST JEALOUSY

Believe the truth. Say it out loud, remember it, and base your life on it: "God wants to give me strength and blessing because I'm fully committed to Him. He wants to make a masterpiece out of me regardless of what there is to start with."

WEEK 10
DAY 1

Dateless, Deprived and Dejected

Stacey was depressed. She felt left out. For the third year in a row, she'd be going to the church youth banquet without a date.

Although she knew there'd be a lot of other unaccompanied females attending, she longed for a nice guy to ask her out for this special occasion. But it wasn't only that. She couldn't remember the last time that one of her girlfriends called to invite her to do something. She had to initiate activities with her friends and keep her ears open so she could tag along for shopping trips and basketball games. She had never been the first one picked for any team—even in kindergarten! Why couldn't she ever be the most important person to somebody?

Do you sometimes feel like Stacey? If you do, you need to know that God has especially picked you for something extremely important. "In him we were chosen, having been predestined according to the plan of him who works out everything in conformity with the purpose of his will, in order that we, who were the first to hope in Christ, might be for the praise of his glory" (Eph. 1:11–12). God chose you to show off to the world how wonderful He is. His plan is first to give you His love, joy and peace so that you can pass it on to others.

Because God is God, He has the capacity to shower all His love and attention on you, His chosen one. You can be the center of His attention just as if no other person existed on this planet. And He can do the same for all His children. The Bible refers to the Church—all who have completely given their lives to Jesus—as the bride of Christ. The reason every girl wants to be a bride is that it means being singled out for such special love and attention. Jesus has the capacity to give the tender caring of a bridegroom to each Christian.

All the acceptance and love in the world is there for the taking. How will you respond? Just as the new wife can decide to ignore or reject the love of her husband and become cold and indifferent, you can keep your distance from God. You can create a world in which you are truly deprived and dejected—and maybe dateless besides. But you *can* learn to receive from God all He has planned to give you.

Try a "date" with Jesus. Take your Bible and go to a nice quiet place and, as you read John 14–17, bask in the love and acceptance of God. Ask Him to fill that hole deep down inside that comes from feeling left out.

MEMORIZE

"I said, 'You are my servant; I have chosen you and have not rejected you.' So do not fear, for I am with you" (Isa. 41:9–10).

VISUALIZE

PERSONALIZE

God is telling me, "________, (your name) you are my servant. I especially picked you and have not given up on you. So don't be afraid, I am with you."

PRAY THE VERSE, APPLYING IT TO YOUR LIFE

Thank you, God, for choosing me as a person you will work through to bring your good news to the world. Thanks for accepting me and not rejecting me. Thanks for being with me so I don't have to be scared.

MEDITATE ON SCRIPTURE

Write this verse down on a card to carry with you throughout the day. Make time to meditate on the verse and apply it to your life. Go to sleep thinking about this verse.

WEEK 10
DAY 2

Self-Examination

1. God loves you and
   _____ a. He accepts you totally.
   _____ b. He wants to change you.
   _____ c. He wants to redeem areas of your life that have been ruined by your sin.
   _____ d. All of the above.

2. I should compare myself with others in an effort to shape up. T F
3. I should enjoy God's acceptance and let Him be the sole judge of my actions. T F
4. God believes in me enough to entrust me with His most important work—that of bringing others to Him. T F
5. Have you been resentful toward God for certain circumstances in your life? ______ If so, explain.

   ____

   What plan does God have for these things you view as disabilities? ____
6. How can you become the center of God's love and attention? ____
7. Do you need to change clothes spiritually? By faith, do you need to take off resentment and put on forgiveness? Do you need to take off anger and put on

gentleness? Describe the change you need to make.

____

8. Is there any desire you have that you need to check with God? ________ What is it? ________________
How do you decide if it is a wishy-washy wish or a true desire of the new you? ________________
9. How many definitions for the grace of God can you list? ________________________
Have you received any of these from God this week? Explain. ________________________
10. Have you been putting into practice the things you learned from this book? ____________ What results have you seen? ________________________
What things are you still waiting for in faith? ________

____

---

1. d. **2.** F. **3.** T. **4.** T. **5.** The plan that God has for things I view as disabilities is that God wants to give me power to overcome them and to use them to build my character. **6.** By spending time in His presence and *receiving* love from Him and by internalizing verses that tell about God's care for me. **7.** Personal. **8.** Check your desires by giving them a lot of time because carnal wishes come and go, also check them with the Bible—no desire that is contrary to the Bible comes from the new you. **9.** Favor, kindness, friendship, God's forgiving mercy, gifts freely bestowed and Christian virtue. **10.** Personal.

PART 6

In Jesus I Am Free

If you hold to my teaching, you are really my disciples. Then you will know the truth and the truth will set you free.

John 8:31–32

WEEK 10
DAY 3

The Freedom Trail Starts Here

Hi! Have you met Phydo, my fluffy French poodle? I have decided that he should be the new liberated dog. Instead of his friendly, cuddly self, he is to become a fierce watchdog in order to remove any doubts he may have about his true masculinity. And I will give him talking lessons so he can become the first dog to break the bark barrier. After all, no dog can be really free unless he can express his desires in words. He will have neither discipline nor restraints. Even if he wishes to jump on the table, he will have the right to express himself in that way.

Wait a minute! Is this freedom? Can you imagine the frustration my poor poodle will experience if someone tries to change his true personality and forces him to attempt the impossible? His lack of discipline will evoke scoldings and rejection from those who should be part of his support group. (Maybe even arsenic poisoning.) Wouldn't it really be more sensible to consult the Person who created Phydo and ask Him what true freedom would be for a French poodle?

What is freedom for you? Do you know? Honest human

beings would have to say no. Those who say they're looking for freedom either exchange one set of chains for another or seem to build for themselves rather formidable prisons. The knowledge that "I did it my way" isn't very comforting when one surveys the mess that has been created.

How do you start on the freedom trail? The Bible tells us: "But the man who looks intently into the perfect law that gives freedom and continues to do this, not forgetting what he has heard, but doing it—he will be blessed in what he does" (James 1:25). God's rules and His advice found in the Bible will correctly define freedom for you. God created you and His plan is to make you totally free to be your true self.

Stop saying things like, "If only my parents weren't so strict, if only I didn't have to attend boring classes every day, if only I could get to a bigger city where something exciting is happening, then I'd feel free." Listen to what God says. His formula for freedom starts on the inside, not on the outside. Because it's not dependent on what others do or say or think, the freedom God gives has a lifetime guarantee. Use God's Word to start on the road to freedom—freedom to be the real you that God created.

WEEK 10
DAY 4

Slave Escapes From Devil's Den

The date is January 1, 1863. Abraham Lincoln has just announced that all slaves in the Confederate states are free. Yet Emmie, a young slave girl whose overseer is especially cruel, continues her drudgery in the cotton fields from sunup until sundown. Why? A war is still going on. Although the North has more men, better technology, and all the resources necessary to win the war, the South has not yet been conquered so that the new law can be enforced.

On April 9, 1865, the day the South surrenders, Emmie is still slaving away. She can't read and, of course, her master is not about to inform her that she is now free. She does hear the news eventually, but even the knowledge that she is no longer a slave doesn't really free Emmie. Neither do changes in the system. Working for pay on the same plantation, she still believes that she is inferior. She is still a slave in her heart. Because of this, her former master treats her no differently than he did before.

Maybe you're an Emmie-type Christian. Even though you've accepted Jesus as your Lord, you don't feel free from Satan and sin and condemnation. The Bible says you *are* free. "For he [God through Jesus] has rescued us from the dominion of darkness and brought us into the kingdom of the Son he loves" (Col. 1:13). You *are* delivered from any power that the devil and his kingdom of darkness tries to exercise over you. But you, like Emmie, may not be experiencing this freedom.

Let's look at what you need to do to live in the liberty that's yours in Jesus. Although Jesus has declared you free because He totally defeated Satan on the cross, the master liar will constantly try to enslave you with chains of deception. You must fight to stay free. Your weapon is the truth found in God's Word. If the devil points out fifteen reasons why this will be a bad day and you feel like a slave to circumstances, you can answer: "But thanks be to God who *always* [even on rainy days when I don't understand the math homework] leads us in triumphal procession in Christ" (2 Cor. 2:14). When Satan whispers, "None of the kids at church really like you," you can point out the truth that Paul wrote to Christians: "For you are all one in Christ" (Gal. 3:28).

Although he'll follow you everywhere with his chains and try to slip them on you when you're not looking, you can be free. The only power the devil has is that of deception. But you must take to heart biblical warnings like these: "Watch and pray so that you will not fall into temptation" (Matt. 26:41); be "watchful and thankful" (Col. 4:2) and "be self-controlled and alert" (1 Pet. 5:8). Don't expect to go on a spiritual vacation. You can't. But don't get discouraged. The devil can never get you as long as you're prepared, and the first piece of armor you must put on is the belt of truth—God's truth, found in His Word.

You don't have to remain an Emmie whose factual freedom has never become an inner reality. Ask Jesus to show you deep in your spirit the freedom you have in Him. Meditate on the verses about freedom in Christ and join the ex-slaves that are escaping from the devil's den.

MEMORIZE

"It is for freedom that Christ has set us free. Stand firm, then, and do not let yourselves be burdened again by the yoke of slavery" (Gal. 5:1).

VISUALIZE

PERSONALIZE

Jesus wants me to experience the freedom He bought for me right now. I, ________, will stick up for my rights as God's child and not let the devil put any of his chains around me again.

PRAY THE VERSE, APPLYING IT TO YOUR LIFE

Dear God, thanks for sending Jesus to die for me in order to make me free. Lord, give me the wisdom to always stand my ground, not letting the devil's lies rob me of the freedom that I have in Jesus.

FIGHT FOR YOUR FREEDOM

List the areas of your life in which you don't feel completely free. Thank Jesus that He has already liberated you. Determine to stand firm in the freedom of Jesus.

WEEK 10
DAY 5

How to Stay Out of Prison and Other Useful Information

Sam had been as excited as anyone else about this stay in Paris—a trip arranged by his French class. It had been a great adventure. They were leaving for home at 6:00 the next morning and this, their last day in Paris, had been designated as a free day. When Lucy decreed that the whole gang should go shopping, no one objected. Because he was nearly broke and he hated to shop, Sam decided to return to the Louvre, one of the greatest museums in the whole world. After all, he could shop at home in Kansas City, but when would he get the opportunity to see so many treasures from the past?

Overconfident of his French (after all, he'd gotten straight *A*'s for three years) and his sense of direction, he left his map in the hotel room. He hopped on a bus only to discover, after a while, that he had no idea where he was going. When he asked for directions, no one seemed to understand him. When an older lady patiently tried to direct him, he couldn't make out what she meant. Soon he found himself in a very poor section of the city, with no idea how to get back to his hotel. He was totally dependent on other people—their captive. He felt that his only hope was to put himself at the mercy of some cab driver even though he knew he didn't have enough money to pay the fare. Sam was frightened. As he flagged down a cab, he pictured himself in a debtor's prison, unable to return to his country.

Without a map or a working knowledge of French, Sam surrendered his freedom. Not knowing the right way to go put him in a jail constructed out of unfavorable circumstances. Similarly, ignorance of the Bible and of scriptural principles can cause you to end up in a spiritual prison.

Jesus said it best. "If you hold to my teaching you are really my disciples. Then you will know the truth, and the truth will set you free" (John 8:31–32). You may object to this by pointing out that Super-Saint Sandy obeys the Ten Commandments better than Moses and doesn't seem to be free. Please remember this important fact: *The freeing truth of God's Word must be applied to your life by the Holy Spirit*, not by people who list twenty-six rules to interpret each verse of Scripture to suit themselves, or by the condemning voice of Satan.

Jesus assured His disciples, "But when he, the Spirit of truth, comes, he will guide you into all truth" (John 16:13). Don't strike out on your own. Although you should listen respectfully to advice of mature Christians and prayerfully bring that counsel before God, asking if it is right for you, don't be bound by what people tell you. Your freedom depends on your following what God says in His Word and letting the Holy Spirit apply that word to each situation in your life.

God's Word is like Sam's map. It will tell you where to go. The Holy Spirit in you, in some ways, can be compared to a mastery of French, which enables you to work out the details in your journey and arrive at the desired destination. Knowing God's truth, letting the Holy Spirit apply that truth to your situation and obeying it conscientiously will keep you out of jail—and lead you into freedom.

MEMORIZE

"I will walk about in freedom, for I have sought out your precepts" (Ps. 119:45).

VISUALIZE

PERSONALIZE

I, ______, will walk around as a free person because I will go after the principles of God's Word.

PRAY THE VERSE, APPLYING IT TO YOUR LIFE

Dear God, thank you that I can live in freedom if I follow your principles. Lord, I'm asking you to guide me as I study your commandments and principles.

PERMIT THE TRUTH TO PENETRATE YOUR PRISON

Take the list you made yesterday (of areas in your life where you sense bondage). Using a concordance or getting the help of a mature Christian who knows the Bible well, write down the verses that apply to these problem areas. Study them prayerfully, asking the Holy Spirit to make these truths real in your life. Let God's Word lead you to freedom.

WEEK 11
DAY 1

You Can Change Your Biography

The leaders of his church considered Bill a model Christian teenager. He came to every service and was careful to avoid everything in the long list of "thou shalt nots" set up as guidelines for the youth. When Bill went off to college he met some neat Christians whose list of prohibitions was considerably shorter, and he adopted their standards. In his sophomore year he made the university track team and started hanging around with the athletes on campus. They were non-Christians and soon Bill became just like them. As news of Bill's activities filtered back to his home church, people were horrified. What had happened to Bill?

This biography could become yours if you don't learn a very important fact about freedom in the Christian life: "Now the Lord is the Spirit, and where the Spirit of the Lord is, there is freedom" (2 Cor. 3:17). Bill's problem was that he got his standards from other people and not from the Holy Spirit. Most of the standards of his church may have been right, but instead of using God's Word and asking the Holy Spirit to establish it in his heart, Bill just went along with the crowd—whether the crowd was good or bad! You'll do the right thing only out of obligation unless you have searched the Scriptures yourself and have let the Holy Spirit show *you* why you should act in a certain way.

For example, Laura honestly enjoyed being witty and sarcastic as she cut people down and rose to stardom among the popular girls at school. They always spent lunch unearthing some new bit of gossip. Whenever her lunchroom leftovers spilled over into home conversation, Laura's mother would chide, "The Bible says that gossip is wrong." Laura would feel a bit guilty and resolve to speak well of everyone. But no one at school laughed at *kind* remarks.

Realizing that her mother would never find out, Laura opted for the center of attention. That is, until she read Matt. 12:36 and found out that Jesus said, "But I tell you that men [and women] will have to give account on the day of judgment for every careless word they have spoken." The words nearly jumped off the page, and sank deep into her heart. The Holy Spirit convicted Laura and she repented of all the harmful things she had said. She was willing to give up her popularity and sit at another table during lunch. She asked the Holy Spirit for His power to help her obey God. Because she was convinced in her heart and relied on the power of the Holy Spirit, she received power to break a sinful habit and became free.

Since many people have flippantly used the idea of the Holy Spirit's guidance as an excuse for their sin, or for ignoring Scripture, some people are afraid of this doctrine. Remembering what Jesus said will prevent you from saying, "But the Holy Spirit told me," as a cop-out for not obeying the Bible: "But the Counselor, the Holy Spirit, whom the Father will send in my name, will teach you all things *and will remind you of everything I have said to you*" (John 14:26).

The Holy Spirit will never lead you contrary to Scripture. To get guidance from the Holy Spirit, read the Scriptures and let the Holy Spirit fill in the details as you obey God's general commands. Don't ignore the advice of other Christians. Instead, ask, "What is the scriptural basis for your believing a Christian should or should not participate in this activity?" Then study these scriptures diligently and ask the Holy Spirit to put the right answer in your heart. Rely on the Holy Spirit to enjoy following God in freedom.

Jesus once asked, "Are you not in error because you do not know the Scriptures or the power of God?" (Mark 12:24). If you carefully study your Bible and receive instruction and power from the Holy Spirit, you'll walk in freedom. The Holy Spirit will apply the Word of God to your life in such a way that it becomes internal conviction. He will give you the strength to obey it. This will change your biography and make it different from Bill's.

MEMORIZE

"Because those who are led by the Spirit of God are sons of God" (Rom. 8:14).

VISUALIZE

PERSONALIZE

As God's child I will be led by the Holy Spirit and not by other people.

PRAY THE VERSE, APPLYING IT TO YOUR LIFE

Dear God, thank you that you lead me by your Spirit. Forgive me for the times I've just gone along with the crowd (Christian or non-Christian) instead of asking you what's right. Please show me if it's God's will for me to _______ (activity you question). Lord, I'm thankful to be your child and I thank you for wanting to lead my life.

MEDITATE ON SCRIPTURE

Copy this material on a card and carry it with you all day using every opportunity to meditate on this verse. Go to sleep thinking about Romans 8:14.

WEEK 11
DAY 2

Do You Watch Reruns on Lucifer's TV Network?

The evening turned out to be a disaster. Glancing at the clock, Shelly realized she might miss the bus. She was going with her literature class to see a stage version of *Julius Caesar.* Attendance was required, since Miss Jones considered this the final review for Monday's test. She was giving zeros to all students who didn't bother to show up.

Running out the door, Shelly noticed a gigantic run in her nylons. There was no time to change. When she boarded the yellow school bus in front of Jefferson High, the only seat left was next to "Crazy Carol." Dressed more or less like a scarecrow, Carol had put on a clown's quantity of makeup for the occasion. "Shelly, do you know you have a run in your nylons?" she boomed.

As Shelly sat down, she noted that Carol could have paid more attention to the deodorant commercials. Shelly couldn't stand sitting with her and gave curt replies to all her nosey questions.

When they arrived at the theater, Shelly ran to catch up with Paula. They purposely chose to sit in a row with only two available seats, thus forcing Carol to sit by herself.

During intermission, Paula confided that she was having terrible problems at home and didn't know which way to turn. It was a perfect chance to witness for Christ, but

Shelly remained silent. The only offer for a ride home came from Harry, the guy she'd been purposely avoiding for weeks. Accepting the ride made her feel guilty.

By the time she walked into the house, Shelly was devastated. "If only I'd gotten ready on time. If only I'd worn nylons without runs. If only I hadn't had to sit next to Carol. If only I'd helped Paula. If only I'd gotten a ride home with John instead of Harry." Then the devil started condemning her. "You're a hopeless Christian. You're supposed to love everyone—even Carol. You didn't witness to Paula and you took advantage of Harry." When she finally fell asleep, she dreamed that Carol was crying because no one loved her, that Paula had committed suicide and Harry had run away from home.

One of the best ways for the devil to handcuff a Christian is by constant haranguing and condemnation. "You did it wrong again. You're a failure. You'll never be a good Christian. You should just quit." But the Bible says, "There is now *no* condemnation for those who are in Christ Jesus" (Rom. 8:1). There is conviction of sin, but there is no condemnation. Shelly needs to realize that her putting popularity above God has opened a door for the devil. She must ask forgiveness for self-centeredness, failure to witness and lack of love. *She needs to be willing to change.* Next, she should receive God's forgiveness and go on like the Apostle Paul: "But one thing I do: Forgetting what is behind and straining toward what is ahead, I press on toward the goal to win the prize for which God has called me heavenward in Christ Jesus" (Phil. 3:13–14). God gave Jonah a second chance to go to Nineveh, and Shelly can pray for another opportunity to show kindness to Carol and to witness to Paula. She can receive power from the Holy Spirit to do these things.

As a Christian, you are free from condemnation. Any attempt by the devil to rehash old failures is his way of torturing you. Resist it. If you did wrong, repent. Then receive forgiveness, and walk in freedom. Watching the devil's reruns of your sins and failures will wipe you out. Instead, fill your mind with words of truth found in the Bible.

MEMORIZE

"Therefore, there is now no condemnation for those who are in Christ Jesus, because through Christ Jesus the law of the Spirit of life set me free from the law of sin and death" (Rom. 8:1–2).

VISUALIZE

PERSONALIZE

I am in Christ Jesus and I, _______, don't have to live under condemnation. Because of Jesus the principles of the life given by the Holy Spirit operate within me and I am free from the principles of sin and death.

PRAY THE VERSE, APPLYING IT TO YOUR LIFE

Dear God, thank you that, because I'm in Jesus, I don't have to put up with condemnation. I will reject the devil's condemning me about _______. Thank you that, as I permit the life of the Holy Spirit to operate in me, I can be free from the law of sin and death.

PONDER THE POWER YOU'VE BEEN GIVEN TO BE FREE

Think about the fact that the law of the Spirit of life—that same power that raised Jesus from the dead—has made you free. Ask God to show you all the power and all the freedom He wants to give you.

WEEK 11
DAY 3

Born Free

Every once in a while, you pick up the newspaper and read a story like this: Henry Smid stole a large amount of money from a German bank when he was a youth. He managed to escape from prison and emigrate to America. Here he formed a prosperous business, retired well-off and enjoyed a fine reputation in the community. Not even his wife knew of his former life of crime. Then the people of Forest Hill were shocked to learn that 90-year-old Mr. Smid had returned to Germany and given himself up to the authorities.

"I was never free on the inside," he remarked. "I just couldn't live with myself any longer." This story could have had a happy ending. The Chancellor of Germany granted Henry a pardon, because the bank Henry stole from is no longer in existence—it was destroyed in World War II. Henry is demanding a jail sentence, however, "so I can die in peace knowing I paid my debt to society."

You can't erase sin any easier than Henry could. You can rationalize your actions, declare yourself forgiven and get everyone else to say that what you're doing is okay. Still, the nagging sense of guilt remains. Without a pardon from Jesus, you'll never be free. Our Savior proclaimed, "So if the Son sets you free, you will be free indeed" (John 8:36). You must confess and forsake every sin—no matter how long ago you did it, no matter how embarrassing that confession might be, regardless of what it will do to your reputation—or your pocketbook.

Then you must *fully accept* the pardon of Jesus. Don't be like the Henry in our story. The devil will try to keep you bound in two ways: First, convincing you not to confess a certain sin and make things right so you can receive forgiveness; second, pursuing you with guilt, condemnation and a desire to do something on your own to merit forgiveness, even after you've confessed your sin and straightened everything out. *Don't let him do it.*

Jesus declared to the people in the synagogue at Nazareth: "He has sent me to proclaim freedom for the prisoners" (Luke 4:18). But He didn't run around letting people out of jail. He freed the Samaritan woman at the well from her ignorance and her sin. He broke the chains of the fear of death for the dying thief on the cross. What is your prison? Jesus can set you free. Your part is to obey and to receive. The truth is that you were born again to be free.

MEMORIZE

"Let them give thanks to the Lord for his unfailing love and his wonderful deeds for men, for he breaks down gates of bronze and cuts through bars of iron" (Ps. 107:15–16).

VISUALIZE

PERSONALIZE

I will thank God for His never-ending love. I will thank Him for the great things He has done. I will be thankful that He performs the impossible and can free me from anything.

PRAY THE VERSE, APPLYING IT TO YOUR LIFE

Dear God, thanks for your unfailing love. Thanks for your wonderful works. Lord, I thank you that you break down gates of bronze and cut through bars of iron and will help me ______ (area in which you need to be free).

MEDITATE ON SCRIPTURE

Make a card like this one to carry with you all day. Think about this verse whenever there is a pause in your activities. Go to sleep meditating on the verse.

WEEK 11
DAY 4

A Slumber Party in a Barn, and Something to Learn

It was a rather unusual event, but the girls from the Bible Club were excited about it. We started to plan a normal slumber party, but one gal suggested that we sleep in the hay mow of a barn outside the city and then prepare breakfast using camp stoves. The idea met with great enthusiasm, and I agreed to chaperone. However, Ketryn,* whose mother had grown up in Eastern Europe, came to talk with me. "My mother doesn't want me to go," she explained. "She thinks that young girls going out in the country for an overnight is a terrible testimony. What will people think?"

"Obey your mother," I counseled. "Although you understand that Americans would not view this activity with suspicion, respect your mother's conscience. It won't hurt you to stay home from one party."

The Apostle Paul explains carefully that we are to be led by God's Spirit individually (and we have seen that the Holy Spirit never guides us contrary to what the Bible teaches), and to enjoy freedom. We don't have to let people build prisons for us with all their taboos and traditions. Nevertheless, 1 Cor. 8:9 tells us: "Be careful, however, that the exercise of your freedom does not become a stumbling block to the weak." There's something much

*Name has been changed.

higher than just being free to enjoy a certain activity: "Nobody should seek his own good, but the good of others" (1 Cor. 10:24).

God wants you to be so free *yourself* that helping others and refraining from offending them comes easily and naturally. Have you ever tried to help a beginner learn to ice skate when you're really not that good yourself? It's a sacrifice. But an excellent skater who has no fear of falling can effortlessly help another. Total freedom is the liberty to follow Jesus completely. "You have been set free from sin and have become slaves to righteousness" (Rom. 6:18). When you're really free, you don't mind giving up your afternoon at the beach to help Mary with her problem. Your heart isn't so set on watching the Super Bowl that you can't listen when Jesus gives other instructions for the day. You're not so fragile that you worry what the other kids think when they see you eating lunch with "Nicholas Nerd."

You see, when you accepted Jesus as your Savior, He remade you—He put His Spirit in you. True freedom is letting that new you who wants only to follow Jesus express its desires. Your flesh (the part of you that is not eternal) may object vigorously, but it can be ignored. Thinking only of selfish desires for your flesh ("I want another chocolate sundae now"; "I can't wait to out-argue that guy and prove I'm right"; "I long to hold that good-looking blond in my arms") makes you a slave to those cravings. True freedom is permitting the real you to follow God.

Jesus told His disciples: "Freely you have received, freely give" (Matt. 10:8). If you keep receiving the freedom Jesus has for you, giving up something to help others won't be a drain on your life. Walking in freedom, Ketryn could dispense with the "Mother, you're-so-old-fashioned" line, and say, "Mother, I respect your opinion and I'll be glad to stay home if you want me to." There was an important lesson to learn from a slumber party in a barn.

MEMORIZE

"You, my brothers, were called to be free. But do not use your freedom to indulge the sinful nature [flesh]; rather, serve one another in love" (Gal. 5:13).

VISUALIZE

PERSONALIZE

I, ________, was destined by Jesus to be free. But I won't use my freedom to pamper my selfishness but will let Jesus make me so free that out of a loving heart I can help other people.

PRAY THE VERSE, APPLYING IT TO YOUR LIFE

Dear God, thanks for wanting me to be free. I realize that I am to be so free that I can serve others with love in my heart. Keep me from defining freedom as getting to do what my body and mind think they want at the moment. Make me so free that I can help others.

BREAK OUT OF YOUR CELL

Is selfishness your cellmate? Unless you allow Jesus to break the attachment you have to enjoying only certain people, owning awesome possessions, and choosing your own activities, you'll never be free to make sacrifices to serve Him.

WEEK 11
DAY 5

Freedom at Bargain Prices

The Larson family is sitting at the dinner table and we're just in time to hear Sue say, "I'm really excited about my new diet. I can eat all I want. I just have to eat the right things. With the 'Delightful Dieting' method I will learn new eating habits and keep the weight off. Pretty soon you'll see me in size ten blue jeans!"

Just then brother Bobby interrupts. "Come on, now. Face reality. In a year or two, you'll be as fat as ever. Soon chocolate candy, cookies, and cake will replace cabbage, cauliflower and carrot sticks. Don't you remember your New Year's resolution to go running every day? Your jogging outfit is as good as new. I seem to recall that the week of hard-boiled eggs and spinach lasted only seventeen hours. Who are you kidding?"

Does Sue's story remind you of similar failures in your life? The ability to "stick with it" seems to be a missing ingredient in modern life. Humans are notably deficient in daily disciplines that form correct habits. It's the very reason that, although Jesus offers liberty to believers, so few Christians are really free. In my opinion, the most important verse in the Bible on Christian freedom is James 1:25: "But the man who looks intently into the perfect law that gives freedom, *and continues to do this, not forgetting what he has heard, but doing it*—he will be blessed in what he does." After you learn some biblical principles of freedom, you must *continually* put them into practice, you must *constantly* renew your mind by meditating on Scripture, and by *daily* obedience maintain your freedom. The devil so successfully uses wrong thought patterns to erase scriptural truth that you must retrain your mind. Whenever you realize that you have violated God's Word, you must confess your sin and turn in the opposite direction.

To illustrate what I mean, let's look in on Erica. Before she accepted Christ, she took drugs, sometimes got drunk, slept with her boyfriend and was rebellious against authority. She had been a Christian two months and God had made miraculous changes in her life. But one Saturday morning, when she was getting ready to go skiing with her friends, her non-Christian mother announced, "This is the day to prove your Christianity. You're staying home and you're cleaning the whole house. You're supposed to obey your mother, you know." At this, Erica exploded in B.C. fashion and stomped out of the house.

After arriving at the ski slopes, it seemed that the devil decided to ride up the chair lift with her. "You're not even a Christian," he scolded; "you'll go back to all your old ways. I've got you and you can never be free."

When they reached the bottom of the run and joined the long line waiting for the chair lift, Kaari noticed that something was wrong and gently asked what the problem was. Erica related the whole story.

"Erica," Kaari reassured, "the Bible says that Jesus has *rescued* you from the devil's kingdom of darkness." (See Col. 1:13.)

"But then, why did I sin?" Erica queried.

"Because Satan deceived you, using old thought patterns to defeat you. But you can act now to clear up the whole mess. First, confess your sin to Jesus. Then I'll drive you home so you can apologize to your mother, and we'll clean the house together. And remember not to ever let the devil condemn you for that sin again."

"But," Erica protested, "that's too much trouble for you. And what will the other kids think?"

"Erica," Kaari emphasized, "following Jesus by confessing and forsaking sin is *much more important* than anything else. Romans 8:14 tells us, 'Those who are led by the Spirit of God'—not by the other kids—'are sons of God.' "

"I know you're right," said Erica, "but how can you be so willing to give up a whole day of skiing to clean house?"

"It's because I really believe that Jesus has made me a new creature with power to obey God and I let the new me follow Jesus. When my body complains, I try not to listen. I prefer to be led by the Spirit. I've found out that if I claim the truth of Scripture and act promptly each time Satan tries to put some chains around me, I can escape. Giving up a day of skiing is a small price to pay for spiritual freedom.

"Erica, it'll cost a lot more if you don't deal with sin immediately. It's a lot harder to win back lost ground than to make a stand now. Actually, one day of housecleaning is nothing. Freedom at this price is a bargain!"

MEMORIZE

"But the man who looks intently into the perfect law that gives freedom, and continues to do this, not forgetting what he has heard, but doing it—he will be blessed in what he does" (James 1:25).

VISUALIZE

PERSONALIZE

But if I, ________, look intently into God's perfect law that gives freedom and keep on studying God's Word, not forgetting what God says and putting it into practice, I will be blessed in what I do.

PRAY THE VERSE, APPLYING IT TO YOUR LIFE

Lord, I believe that your rules are perfect and that they give freedom. Help me to take your Word seriously, to constantly study and obey it daily so I can receive your blessing.

MEDITATE ON SCRIPTURE

Make a card like this one to take with you today. Whenever you can, review the verse and think about its meaning. Drift off to dreamland repeating the verse in your mind.

WEEK 12
DAY 1

Self-Examination

1. Who is the only one who can define what freedom is for you? ______
2. What's the problem if you're a Christian and don't really feel free? ______
______
3. What should be your reason for participating in a certain activity or for not taking part in it? ______
______
4. What is the only power the devil has against a Christian? ______
5. There is now no ______ for those who are in Christ Jesus.
6. Have you let the devil put any chains around you? ______ Explain ______
How can you get free? ______
7. Have you started to adopt new-creature mentality? ______ Tell about changes you've seen in your life because of it. ______
8. God accepts you just as you are in order to do what? ______
9. What part of your life needs to be redeemed and restored? ______ Are you holding on in faith and expecting God to make something good out of the situation that seems so bad? ______

10. Have you been asking Jesus for His grace every day—or nearly every day? ________ Do you receive from Him whatever you need to face each new situation? ____

---

1. God, the one who made you. **2.** It might be that you're ignorant of all Jesus has to give you. Maybe you've accepted Satan's chains of deception. Perhaps you haven't permitted the freeing truth of God's Word to be applied to your life by the Holy Spirit. **3.** Because you have searched the Scriptures yourself and have permitted the Holy Spirit to guide you in your conduct. **4.** Deception. **5.** Condemnation. **6.–7.** Personal. **8.** To change me. **9.–10.** Personal.

PART 7

In Jesus I Am One With Other Christians

So in Christ we who are many form one body.

Romans 12:5

WEEK 12
DAY 2

Now Offering Eternal Life Membership!

Numb and tearless, only because she had no energy left to cry, Kay took one last look at the open grave and the casket that contained the body of her mother. She permitted her uncle to help her to the car.

It was as if a hidden movie projector that had no off button insisted on replaying the tragic events of the past four days: the call over the school loudspeaker, "Would Kay Brown please come to the office immediately"; the tears in her aunt's eyes as she told Kay that her mother had been in a serious car accident; the hours in the intensive care waiting room hoping against hope; the nurse coming out to announce her mother's death. Then came the endless parade of people offering their sympathy, funeral arrangements, and the sharp pain that came each time she thought of things in her life that were gone forever. No longer could she get her mother's opinion on what clothes to buy, or eat the homemade cinnamon rolls her mother made each Tuesday, or receive her mom's comfort after a hard day at school.

For Kay, the death of her mother also meant losing all

sense of belonging. She was an only child, and her father had abandoned Kay and her mother ten years before. Having been invited to live with her aunt and uncle, she wondered if she could adapt to living with four cousins so different from herself. She didn't seem to fit anywhere.

Even if you haven't been separated from anyone by death, you may sometimes identify with Kay. Maybe you're the "foreigner in the family." Perhaps you experience that "fifth-wheel" feeling wherever you go. Do you ever wonder where you can feel accepted? If you've surrendered your life to Jesus and have received new life from Him, you belong—first of all to Jesus and then to God's forever family.

Jesus discussed this with His Father just before He was crucified: "I pray also for those who will believe in me through their [the apostles'] message, that all of them may be one, Father, just as you are in me and I am in you. May they also be in us" (John 17:20–21). It's not like Jesus was just praying that Christians would get along, He was also describing what happens when a person believes in Jesus so deeply that he acts on that belief and receives new life.

An illustration from the physical realm may be helpful. The union of your parents put your life within your mother and put life from your parents in you. Because your brothers and sisters were formed the same way, you have a special unity with them and we say you're part of a family. It's the same way spiritually. Jesus lives in your heart, but in an equally unexplainable way, you are in Jesus, Jesus is in the Father and those who have experienced the miracle of this new birth are united in Christ. Jesus explained to His disciples: "Because I live, you also will live. On that day you will realize that I am in my Father, and you are in me, and I am in you" (John 14:19–20).

"That day" refers to the coming of the Holy Spirit at Pentecost. Jesus was telling the disciples that through the revelation of the Holy Spirit they would realize their position. Christ was in them. They were in Christ. Christ was in the Father and because of that they were one with all other believers in Christ. What a wonderful unity! And it's something that death can't touch. Jesus is alive forevermore. Christians who have died and gone to heaven are still part of the family and they're waiting for us to join them so we can continue to enjoy our oneness in Christ for all eternity.

Because Christians don't all look alike or think alike or have the same last name or all get together at once for a family reunion, we sometimes forget about our brothers and sisters in Christ. When misunderstandings and differences of opinion seem to divide us, we must remember that God has offered us eternal life membership in His family—and you can't just switch families whenever you wish. With the security of belonging comes responsibility.

WEEK 12
DAY 3

Everybody Needs One Body!

Steve's parents had just had another fight.

Predictable as a TV rerun, it had begun when Steve's mother announced that she had called an interior decorator to get an estimate for completely redoing the living room and buying all new furniture. Steve's father had exploded and decreed that his hard-earned money would not be spent so frivolously. Steve's mother then countered: "If that's the way you're going to treat me, I'm leaving." She slammed the bedroom door and proceeded to pack her suitcase.

Opening the front door to get the evening paper, Steve's father mumbled, "Well, it sure would cut down on living expenses." Then he sat down in his favorite chair and switched on the evening news.

After giving his father time to calm down, Steve took advantage of a commercial. "Dad," he began, "I've saved all the money I need. Please let me go on the youth retreat this weekend."

His father used his "this-is-the-last-word" tone of voice: "I don't want you mixed up with religious fanatics. You know that. Don't even bother asking me if you can participate in church activities. The answer is *no*."

Just then his mother appeared with her suitcase in her hand, "Your father is right. Too much religion ruins people." And she left to spend the night with her mother.

Steve felt totally alone. He had accepted Christ, but his parents forbade him to go to church and did everything possible to prevent him from having Christian friends. The only thing his parents seemed to agree on was that there was no God and people involved in Christianity were ignorant, superstitious and weak. Steve desperately needed someone to talk to.

Do you sometimes feel like Steve? Remember, you are not alone. You are part of the body of Christ. Because of that fact, there is literally an army of people who care for you and want to help. However, there are certain individuals that God wants to especially use in your life. Pray until God leads you to some of these people.

Don't let pride or timidity keep you from contacting another Christian for help. Write that letter, make that phone call, or just walk up to a brother or sister in Christ and say, "Please pray with me." The Bible commands us, "Carry each other's burdens, and in this way you will fulfill the law of Christ" (Gal. 6:2). This means that Christians are to share their problems with each other. How else could we carry each other's burdens?

Because humans make mistakes, are sometimes too busy to take time for you, and are capable of misunderstanding your intentions or giving wrong advice, your complete confidence must always be in Jesus—not in any person. But God intended for some Christian to put loving arms around you when you're hurting. He planned for you to hear soothing words from a member of God's family. He has arranged that a group of Christian friends would come to your aid in time of crisis. His blueprint is described in Eph. 4:15–16: "Instead, speaking the truth in love, we will in all things grow up into him who is the Head, that is, Christ. From him the whole body, joined and held together by every supporting ligament, grows and *builds itself up in love, as each part does its work.*" Everybody needs one body!

MEMORIZE

"So that there should be no division in the body, but that its parts should have equal concern for each other. If one part suffers, every part suffers with it; if one part is honored, every part rejoices with it" (1 Cor. 12:25–26).

VISUALIZE

PERSONALIZE

I am part of the body of Christ. I shouldn't let anything divide me from another Christian. I should be concerned about other Christians and should share my problems so they can be concerned for me. I will be part of the sufferings and victories of other Christians.

PRAY THE VERSE, APPLYING IT TO YOUR LIFE

Dear God, thank you for making me a part of the body of Christ. Help me be a peacemaker and teach me how to care about other Christians and to receive care from them. Show me how to empathize and share their triumphs and defeats.

SHARE TRIALS AND JOYS WITH OTHER CHRISTIANS THIS WEEK

If you're hurting, ask God to show you another Christian who could be of help to you. If you're walking on water, ask God to show you another person you can help.

WEEK 12
DAY 4

Pig Pens and Peace

Jill and Krystal had been close friends for two years. Because they attended the same school and the same church, they had similar interests and doing things together seemed only natural.

Then it happened. Jill accepted a date with Dan, and soon they were going out rather steadily. Since Krystal had had a well-publicized crush on Dan for two years, she considered him her property. She felt that her best friend had betrayed her by stealing "her" guy. Krystal wouldn't even talk to Jill. Meanwhile Jill did nothing to try to straighten things out since she felt she had done nothing wrong. They both sang, "We are one in the Spirit" in the same choir. They repeated "forgive us our debts as we forgive our debtors" while sitting in the same row, but they weren't on speaking terms.

Have you ever been a Jill or a Krystal? What do you do about a situation like that? The first step is to meditate on Scripture and to claim the fact that you are one in Christ with the Christian you're having trouble getting along with. "For He himself [Jesus] is our peace, who has made the two one and has destroyed the barrier, the dividing wall of hostility" (Eph. 2:14).

Next, you put Rom. 14:19 into practice: "Let us therefore make every effort to do what leads to peace and to mutual edification." You are responsible to work hard for

Christian unity—whether or not the fault was yours. First go to the person to humbly ask forgiveness. Or if you don't know what you've done, ask the person how you've offended him or her. If the person refuses to forgive you, pray for that person every day. Ask God what extra special thing you can do for the person to demonstrate your love and concern. It might mean buying a little gift, going out of your way to help, or waiting until God opens a special opportunity for you to serve that person.

If you have a clear title to one hundred acres of beautiful wooded shoreline property, it's yours. You have a right to enjoy all that fresh air, inspiring scenery, the peace and quiet. If squatters come in and erect tarpaper shacks, if someone starts building a brick factory on your beach, and another person tries to fence in a piece of your land to pasture hogs, you must fight for your legal rights.

In the spiritual realm it's no different. Jesus has already bought a clear title for peace among Christians, paying for it with His blood. Don't allow the devil to set up his pig pen on your property.

As strange as it may seem, Christians must continue to actively fight to keep the unity that Jesus purchased for them. If there is strain between you and another Christian, it's your responsibility to do everything possible to resolve it.

MEMORIZE

"Therefore, if you are offering your gift at the altar and there remember that your brother has something against you, leave your gift there in front of the altar. First go and be reconciled to your brother; then come and offer your gift" (Matt. 5:23–24).

VISUALIZE

PERSONALIZE

If I am singing in the choir, listening to the sermon, or taking the offering and I remember that my friend has something against me, even if it's not my fault, I must go seek his forgiveness and then come back to church.

PRAY THE VERSE, APPLYING IT TO YOUR LIFE

Dear God, I know it's wrong to try to offer any service or sacrifice to you if there is unforgiveness in my heart. I forgive ________ (person who is hard to love) and I'm willing to go to ________ and apologize and ask for forgiveness. *(Don't pray this one if you don't mean it.)*

FIGHT FOR PEACE

Do your part to be on good terms with everyone. If you sense that someone has something against you—even if you think they're to blame—go to that person and try to clear things up.

WEEK 12
DAY 5

God Is Big Enough to Protect Himself!

Greg winced. "Bertha Bible-Banger" was at it again.

He could hear her at the next lunch table loudly reading long passages from the King James Bible and telling amused students that they were going to hell. He was certain that after "Bertha's Blitz," no student at Kennedy High would think that sanity and Christianity could go together. Although he had to admit that she was bold, Greg felt no bond of Christian unity with that heavy-set, sloppily dressed "this-is-a-recorded-message-from-heaven" broadcaster. He and five other Christians had wanted to organize a special youth rally and invite kids from school—but that was before "Big Bertha" appeared on the scene.

Have you ever felt like Greg did? How do you react when a warning sign *"Danger—Saints at Work"* seems necessary? First of all start with this fact: "The body is a unit, though it is made up of many parts; and though all its parts are many, they form one body. So it is with Christ. For we were all baptized by one Spirit into one body" (1 Cor. 12:12–13). The parts of your physical body don't avoid each other; they learn to work together. If your left foot hurts, the body makes some adjustments in the way it walks. If your mouth says something that offends another person, the brain tries to figure out a formula for a peace treaty. How marvelously the body compensates for loss of hearing or loss of sight!

If you really believe you're part of the body of Christ, you'll try to fill in for the lack of discernment and mistakes of other Christians. First, you'll pray for them and gently try to help them change. Then you'll ask God if there is anything you can do or say to remove a wrong impression or smooth over a rough situation.

However, the most important thing to remember is that God runs the universe and His plans don't get messed up just because someone fumbles the ball, or talks out of turn, or uses poor judgment. The credibility of Christianity is not on your shoulders. *You can trust God* to use methods you despise or think are most inappropriate. The Apostle Paul gives us guidelines we better heed. He was talking about men who went on preaching tours from selfish motives with the purpose of stirring up trouble for him when he was in prison. His attitude? "But what does it matter? The important thing is that in every way, whether from false motives or true, Christ is preached, and because of this I rejoice" (Phil. 1:18). Paul trusted God.

Once, God showed me specifically that He used methods I didn't approve of. As a leader of the Bible club in the high school where I taught, I was happy to see Curt,* a tenth grader, accept Christ and become a regular at our meetings. However, the ways Curt chose to display his Christianity made me uncomfortable—I didn't want to lose the good working relationship we had with the school administration. But then one day the counselor talked to me and asked if she could send other kids to our club. The reason? Curt (who I thought might be blowing our image) had changed so much for the better that she wanted to help other kids. I didn't know Curt before he became a Christian!

God is big enough to protect himself—and the reputation of Christianity in the whole world. Give that job to Him and enjoy being part of the body of Christ.

---

*Name has been changed.

MEMORIZE

"Now, you are the body of Christ, and each of you is part of it" (1 Cor. 12:27).

VISUALIZE

PERSONALIZE

I am a member of the body of Christ and so is every other true Christian throughout the world—even if we don't all go at things the same way.

PRAY THE VERSE, APPLYING IT TO YOUR LIFE

Dear God, thank you for making me a part of the body of Christ. Thank you that ________ (Christian person who you think is not very cool) is also a part of the body and is just as important as I am.

PUT YOUR FINGER IN THE DIKE!

Ask God to give you His perspective on His work instead of becoming embarrassed and upset when other Christians mess things up. Also ask Him to show you how you can compensate for the errors of other members of the body of Christ.

WEEK 13
DAY 1

Saved, Sanctified—
*and **Petrified***

Janelle met Rosa in biology class. When the teacher started telling the class that a big explosion had caused the universe, Rosa raised her hand and asked, "Mr. Jones where did the materials for the big bang come from, and what caused the explosion?"

The teacher glared at her, "Rosa, I thought you were an intelligent young lady. You certainly don't believe the Genesis fairy tale, with Adam and Eve and the snake, do you?"

"I sure do," replied Rosa. "God did just as big a miracle in my own life when he saved me out of drugs and prostitution."

The teacher was stunned and everyone stared at Rosa. Janelle smiled at her, and rushed to her side after class explaining that she too was a Christian. They became fast friends, but soon some problems developed. Rosa believed things that Janelle's church labeled "wrong doctrine." And Rosa had trouble accepting some things Janelle affirmed to be true. When Rosa invited Janelle to her church for a special crusade, Janelle's parents wouldn't allow her to go.

Has the fact that God's children don't all think alike ever bothered you? Do you look for ways to handle Rosa-Janelle situations, or do you avoid the problem by just sticking with people from your denomination or your church? Since all true Christians are part of the body of Christ, we need to seek biblical solutions when differences of opinion try to divide us.

First of all, we should take seriously what Jesus told His followers, "All men will know that you are my disciples if you love one another" (John 13:35)—not, if all of you believe exactly the same thing. No human is infallible. When we get to heaven, I'm sure we'll all discover that we've had some wrong doctrine. However, God's supernatural love is available so we can truly appreciate each other. It's wonderful to experience love so strong, that the differences no longer matter.

Then we need to remember that perfect doctrine comes only from God. "Let God be true, and every man a liar" (Rom. 3:4). It wasn't a system of belief in outline form that Jesus gave us when He left for heaven but a promise: "But when he, the Spirit of truth, comes, he will guide you into all truth" (John 16:13). It's the Holy Spirit that will instruct us and tell us what the Bible means—not modern science or current public opinion. Other problems often occur when people attempt to add something to the Bible. We find a good principle in 1 Cor. 4:6: "Do not go beyond what is written."

How could Rosa and Janelle apply these principles to their situation? They need to continually receive God's love for each other. Both of them could learn a great deal if they went to their church leaders to ask for the Bible verses to support church beliefs. Each could listen as the other gave passages of Scripture for investigation. Both could diligently study the Bible and ask the Holy Spirit to give them light. Both could be willing to change if their beliefs could not be supported by God's Word. And their love for each other could increase in spite of differences that still remained.

All of us must be willing to learn from other members of the body of Christ. Having had the opportunity to fellowship with many different Christian groups, I have learned something important. Whatever scripture a group completely believes and applies becomes their strength.

On the other hand, the verses they ignore or reject are reflected in weaknesses in their lives. Determine to be a Christian who loves and learns from all members of the body of Christ. Saints who consider themselves "saved, sanctified and petrified" are missing out on a whole lot.

MEMORIZE

"All Scripture is God-breathed and is useful for teaching, rebuking, correcting and training in righteousness" (2 Tim. 3:16).

VISUALIZE

PERSONALIZE

I, ________, determine not to leave any Bible verse out of my doctrine—even if it completely blows my neat system. I will remember to use Scripture if I try to correct another Christian—not my logic or tradition. I will change my ideas to conform with the Bible.

PRAY THE VERSE, APPLYING IT TO YOUR LIFE

Dear God, thank you for your Word—every verse of it. Help me not to ignore any passages that don't fit my pattern. Help me to take correction when it is backed up with Scripture and not to try to change anyone else unless I have Bible verses to prove my point.

MEDITATE ON SCRIPTURE

Make a card like this one. Meditate on the verse every chance you get. Ask God to make the verse real to you. Think about the verse as you go to sleep.

WEEK 13
DAY 2

Are You Looking for a Compliment From Jesus?

Brittany looked over the kitchen—mountains of dirty dishes, red Kool-Aid spilled all over the floor, melted ice cream dripping from the counter—disaster city. Carmen, who was sweeping the meeting room floor, spoke her mind. "Those who can't do anything else get to clean up, right?"

Renting the Y for a youth group Valentine's party (with the purpose of evangelizing unsaved friends) was a really good idea. The event had been a huge success. Committees had been formed. Those with artistic talent made the decorations and invitations. The program was planned by the musically gifted and good public speakers. Only kids with cars could provide transportation, while creative individuals came up with the games. All leftovers formed the cleanup committee with Brittany, the most responsible, in charge. Except for Carmen, everyone on her committee had an excuse for having to leave early. So the two girls had to do all the work by themselves. That night Brittany wished she were different—a person who wouldn't automatically be assigned to the cleanup committee.

Have you ever had a case of the "I'm-not-very-important-to-anybody" blues? It comes from reverting to the standards of the world instead of accepting the biblical teaching that all members of the body of Christ have equal status. (When believers fall into making heroes out of certain Christian singers or speakers, and act as though only prominent people count, it's easy to contract the disease.) The cure is standing on Scripture: "But God has combined the members of the body and has given greater honor to the parts that lacked it" (1 Cor. 12:24). God gives great honor to members of the cleanup committee. God doesn't sponsor talent contests and give prizes. He grades on faithfulness. "Now it is required that those who have been given a trust must prove faithful" (1 Cor. 4:2). The fact is that as you responsibly fulfill the duties assigned, you acquire new abilities. But to God, your attitudes and motives far outweigh accomplishments.

The Gospels record some of the compliments that Jesus gave. Have you ever noticed who received them? He commended Nathaniel (one of the less prominent disciples), saying, "Here is a true Israelite, in whom there is nothing false" (John 1:47). He noticed a poor widow who gave God all she had. He complimented a centurion (a despised Roman) on his great faith. And He told people that John the Baptist, who willingly gave up all his disciples to Jesus and who was in prison for speaking out on moral issues, was a great man.

If you tend to become discouraged because of your "behind the scenes ministry," remember that Jesus notices what you do. He also sees your motives.

Are you looking for a compliment from Jesus, or are you going to be bound to the opinions of those around you?

MEMORIZE

"Whoever wants to become great among you must be your servant, and whoever wants to be first must be your slave—just as the Son of Man did not come to be served, but to serve" (Matt. 20:26–28).

VISUALIZE

PERSONALIZE

If I want to be a great Christian I must be willing to be on the cleanup committee and ______ (necessary job you hate). If I want to be a leader, I must attend to the needs of other people including ______ (helping person who doesn't show proper appreciation). Jesus set the example. He didn't come to be waited on. He gave himself for others.

PRAY THE VERSE, APPLYING IT TO YOUR LIFE

Thank you for teaching me that doing unnoticed work to help others is important. Thanks for helping me see that I must be willing to spend my life serving other Christians—no matter what talents I have. Thank you for being the perfect example of a life of service.

SPONSOR YOUR OWN SEMINAR ON SERVICE

Ask God how you can be a servant today. Volunteer for one of the less glamorous jobs and do it for Jesus. Contribute to the body of Christ by your humility.

WEEK 13
DAY 3

Part of the Package Deal

Miss Burns was young, a lot of fun, and as good a speech teacher as anyone could ask for. Liz was one of four Christian students in the class. All of them were working together to try to win Miss Burns to Jesus. They took advantage of speech topics like "The Best Thing I Ever Did Was" to talk to the class about their faith in Jesus. Jan asked Miss Burns to come to church with her, and Liz had invited her home for dinner. Miss Burns expressed interest in studying the Bible.

Then it happened! Dustyn was caught using a crib sheet on the semester exam. "I thought you were a Christian!" Miss Burns exploded. "I thought Christians were supposed to do what's right. I don't ever want anybody talking to me about accepting Jesus or following any other religion. I'm an atheist, but I'm honest. I don't believe in God, but never in my life have I cheated on a test. From now on any speeches on religion receive an automatic *F*."

Liz was furious. How could Dustyn have done such a thing? How could he have brought dishonor on the name of Christ and on the Christians at Lakeview High? When the next speech topic was announced—"Why I Have a Great Future"—Liz thought about what she could have said if it hadn't been for Dustyn. She even had a hard time being friendly to him. It seemed that the resentment inside her was about to boil over.

Every Christian encounters the problem Liz faced. What do *you* do when the sin of another Christian messes things up for you and a whole bunch of other people?

First of all, you must remember that the person who sinned is still part of the body of Christ, and your primary obligation is to completely forgive him or her. God's Word declares: "But if you do not forgive men their sins [no matter what they've done], your Father will not forgive your sins" (Matt. 6:15).

Next, just let God be God. Pray that He will repair the unfair damage done to His reputation and yours. Pray that He will provide another opportunity for the non-Christian affected to see that Jesus really does manufacture new creations. Ps. 37:6 is a promise: "He will make your righteousness shine like the dawn, the justice of your cause like the noonday sun." Then instead of giving the person a piece of *your* mind decide which piece of *God's* mind you should dish out: either Gal. 6:1: "Brothers, if someone is caught in a sin, you who are spiritual should restore him gently. But watch yourself, or you also may be tempted," or 1 John 5:16: "If anyone sees his brother commit a sin that does not lead to death, he should pray and God will give him life."

It all starts with forgiveness. Don't let the devil convince you that you're justified in not forgiving a Christian whose sin has caused great harm to others in the body. "Forgiving each other just as Christ forgave you" (Eph. 4:32) is the way the body operates. Forgiving others isn't just an optional extra—it's part of the package deal along with everlasting love, purpose for living and pardon for all your sins.

MEMORIZE

"Above all, love each other deeply, because love covers over a multitude of sins" (1 Pet. 4:8).

VISUALIZE

PERSONALIZE

The most important thing is that I love all other Christians so much that I erase their sins against me and against others with that love.

PRAY THE VERSE, APPLYING IT TO YOUR LIFE

Dear God, thanks for showing me that my love for other Christians is more important than my Christian service. I determine to love _______ (a Christian whose sin has caused a lot of trouble) and forgive him or her as you have forgiven me.

MEDITATE ON SCRIPTURE

Take a card like this with you today. Whenever you have the opportunity, review the verse and let its message sink in. Go to sleep thinking about the verse.

WEEK 13
DAY 4

Love Is Contagious—Start an Epidemic!

Loretta looked around uneasily as she entered the small white church. She sat down near the back. No one greeted her and several people stared. After a couple of songs and scripture reading, the Sunday school superintendent asked people to go to their classes. Loretta didn't know where the senior high class met, but she spotted a girl she had noticed in her English class and decided to follow her.

The teacher greeted Loretta formally and asked for her name, but no one seemed genuinely glad to see her. Loretta was black, and because of her father's job, her family had moved to an all-white community. She had expected a rather cool reception at school, but it hurt her deeply that kids who were supposed to be her brothers and sisters in Christ refused to fully accept her.

Unfortunately, Loretta's situation isn't unique. There are many Christians who feel rejected and left out for various reasons. Being a different color, speaking with an accent, not being able to dress as well as the others, being considered less-than-cool, and having different interests are some of those reasons. How can you deal with disapproval from other Christians?

You always start with the fact of Scripture: "You [Christian] have taken off your old self with its practices and have put on the new self, which is being renewed in knowledge in the image of its Creator. Here there is no Greek or Jew, circumcised or uncircumcised, barbarian, Scythian, slave, or free, but Christ is all, and is in all" (Col. 3:11). The fact is that as a true Christian you've taken off the old self that allows others to make you feel inferior. You've put on a new self that is as important in the body of Christ as anybody else. It's just that you have to constantly adopt God's mind-set to remember truth and reject icy stares, lack of consideration, unkind words, unfair judgments and just plain prejudice.

If your mind is continually on Jesus, you can be used by God to bring other Christians to the realization that those who know Jesus are meant to be one big happy family in which there is overflowing love for one another. In God's family it doesn't matter if you are black or white, rich or poor, best-all-around, Ordinary Oscar, Brian the Brain, or Macho Matt. Love is contagious. If you allow God to give you love to display to those who reject you, they'll catch some of it too. Wouldn't you like to be the one who started the love epidemic?

MEMORIZE

"You are all sons of God through faith in Christ Jesus. . . . There is neither Jew nor Greek, slave nor free, male nor female, for you are all one in Christ Jesus" (Gal. 3:26–28).

VISUALIZE

PERSONALIZE

I am a son/daughter of God because I have faith in Christ Jesus. In Jesus there is neither black nor white, Asian nor Chicano. There is neither executive nor factory worker, male nor female. I'm one with every other Christian, and we're all one in Jesus.

PRAY THE VERSE, APPLYING IT TO YOUR LIFE

Dear God, thanks that you're my Father because I have faith in Jesus Christ. Thank you that nothing really matters—my race, my position, my ability, my sex—because I'm united with all other true Christians in Jesus.

GIVE YOURSELF A "LOVE-ONE-ANOTHER-AS-I-HAVE-LOVED-YOU" TEST

List the names of the Christians you know whom you don't really love. Add the type of person you wouldn't love even if you had the opportunity. Then ask God's forgiveness for disobeying His command and appropriate His never-ending supply of unfailing love to give out to *everyone* in God's family.

WEEK 13
DAY 5

Self-Examination

1. Why are you a brother or a sister to every other Christian? ______
2. If your friend is mad at you and you're innocent, what should you do? ______
3. If your friend is angry with you because you said some harsh words, what should you do? ______
4. What should you do if some Christian really blows it and spoils things for other Christians? ______
5. What should you do if a person who is a born-again Christian challenges something you have been taught? ______
6. There is *never* a time when I'm justified in not forgiving another person. T F
7. How do you handle lack of acceptance by other Christians? ______
8. Did the devil put any chains around you this week? Explain. ______ How did you get free? If you didn't get free yet, how are you going to get free? ______

 ______
9. What did you wear this week?
   ____ a. Forgiveness.
   ____ b. Patience.
   ____ c. Love.
   ____ d. Other (specify).

10. What did you ask God for this week?
_____ a. Mercy.
_____ b. Friendship.
_____ c. Kindness.
_____ d. Favor.

---

1. The Bible teaches that we're all one in Christ. I am in Christ and Christ is in me. This is also true of every other Christian. We were formed the same way—made out of the same stuff so to speak—and that makes us part of the same family. **2.** I should go to ask that person how come he or she feels offended and then try to smooth out the relationship. **3.** I should go and ask the person to forgive me and then do all I can to heal the relationship. **4.** First I forgive him or her. Then I pray that he or she will see God's truth and if God leads me to do it, I gently try to restore the person to correct thinking, using Scripture to back up what I say. **5.** I should ask the person who is challenging me for scripture to back up his or her views. Then I ask someone in my church for Bible verses to support the teaching I've received. Next I ask the Holy Spirit to guide me and show me truth as I study these Scripture passages. **6.** T. **7.** I stand on the scripture that all members of Christ's body are equal and because of that no one can make me feel inferior. I start a love epidemic. **8.**— **10.** Personal.